I Can.
You Can Too!

by

Mamie McCullough

Honor Books
Tulsa, Oklahoma

All Scripture quotations, unless otherwise indicated, are taken from the *New King James Version*. Copyright © 1979, 1980, 1982 by Thomas Nelson, Inc. Used by permission. All rights reserved.

2nd Printing

I Can. You Can Too!
ISBN 1-56292-572-5
Copyright © 1997 by Mamie McCullough
305 Spring Creek Village
Dallas, TX 75248

Published by Honor Books, Inc.
P. O. Box 55388
Tulsa, Oklahoma 74155

Printed in the United States of America. All rights reserved under International Copyright Law. Contents and/or cover may not be reproduced in whole or in part in any form without the express written consent of the Publisher.

This book is dedicated to the greatest children

any mother was ever blessed with —

my Patti, Brian, and Jennifer.

If others learn as much about love

from reading this book as I have learned from you,

the world will be a better place for all of us.

Contents

Acknowledgments

If I were to thank everyone
involved in the writing of this book,
this section might well be longer
than the following pages, so I will refrain
from trying to mention everyone by name.

I thank God for allowing me the opportunity
to tell my story. I thank Zig and Jean Ziglar
for their support of me and my family.
I thank my family for their patience, support, and love.
And I thank you for reading these pages.

Foreword 1

History books dutifully record the fact that all great ideas, movements, organizations, and corporations start in the mind of one person. I believe future history books will include the name of Mamie McCullough, who started the "I CAN" program in our school systems. Her name will be included because this program is making a positive difference in the lives of millions of students and teachers and will ultimately make a difference in America's future.

Your question might well be, who is this Mamie McCullough who, just a few years ago, was a skinny, awkward, insecure, buck-toothed teenager with a breathing problem that caused red blotches to break out all over her face when she was the least bit flustered? How could anybody with those difficulties become a charming, attractive, witty, loving human being who is today one of America's most articulate, entertaining, and inspiring speakers and communicators?

Now for fear I paint too bleak a picture of the way she was, let me point out that she did have many important things going for her. She had great faith, a willingness to work, a determination to succeed, a thirst for knowledge, a curiosity about life, and a desire to use what God had given her. She also had a loving, supportive, Christian mother. And the thought you should bear in mind is that the qualities that have taken her to the top are already in you — or they can be developed.

Mamie McCullough tells how she did it in her heartwarming book, *I Can. You Can Too!* It's one of those "must read" books for all who have ever seriously wondered if they really have what it takes to do big things in life. "Miss Mamie" spells out in precise terms the background from which she comes, the difficulties she encountered, the obstacles she overcame, and the heartaches and disappointments that were so numerous in her life. She tells you how she "won" and, more importantly, how you can win.

You'll read this book amid laughter, tears, excitement, despair, exhilaration, and every other known human emotion. When you finish you'll say, "I'm glad this book was written. I'm grateful that somehow it came into my hands." It's a winner — and you're gonna love it!

Zig Ziglar
Dallas, Texas

Foreword 2

Mamie Darlington McCullough's life is a dramatic example of the meaning of Christian education within the framework of the noblest ideals, morals, spiritual values, and intellectual achievement. Her desires and motivation have carried her on the wings of faith to unprecedented success. Her voice needs to be heard.

With her faith in God, her love for people, and her unquestioned integrity, she has taught all of us who know her best the rich legacy of realizing one's full potential within the context of personal freedom and the most coveted virtues of faith, hope, and love.

Guy Newman
President Emeritus
Howard Payne University

I Can.
You Can Too!

I CAN.
YOU CAN
TOO!

*S*cientists have proven that it is aerodynamically impossible for the bumblebee to fly. Its body is too heavy, and its wings are too light. You've probably read about this phenomenon before. However, the bumblebee doesn't read — it just flies!

The bumblebee can be an inspiration to each of us. Napoleon's officers wore a bee on their uniforms as a symbol of courage. Today, many athletic teams wear a bee on their uniforms to symbolize their ability to overcome the impossible. At least one company I have spoken for has adopted the bee as part of their logo to show they bee-lieve.

Professionals don't need to be told, but they're glad to be reminded. The dozen "bees" on the pages that follow will remind you and me to be all that God wants and allows us to be.

Today is the best day of my life because I decided it would be. Now, I don't know who you are or where you are today in your life, but I hope you got up this morning saying, "This is the best day of my life." And I hope you choose to *make* today the best day of your life.

I haven't always felt this way. I grew up thinking there was no hope for me, and without hope life seems unbearable. As I have continued to grow (not just go) through life, however, I have learned some very important lessons. My goal is to share the joys and heartaches of my life so that you can learn from my experiences. I want to tell my story because, in many ways, my story is your story. I believe that there is something in these pages that will cause you to say, "I can relate to that. If she can do it, I can too!"

— THE BEGINNING —

I was born Mamie Claire Darlington on April 3, 1939, in rural south Georgia. Three years later, we moved to a little town called Dixie, Georgia, which is about 95 miles south of Plains. In Dixie we bought a small, two-story home that had never had a coat of paint, paying ten dollars a month. Even though I had a mother with strong character and courage who pulled us through rough times, I often felt I was living in a hopeless situation. I thought that because my mother had no education, because I had so many brothers and sisters, and because I was born at the time I was, I would never amount to anything.

But you know, when or where you were born does not determine your success. Success is determined by what is "inside." I believe it was General Douglas MacArthur who wisely said that security is an inside job. So many of us waste a lifetime blaming our inadequacies and lack of determination on our parents or our circumstances. We say, "If things had been different," "If I were younger or older or taller," or "If I had been born in the city instead of a small rural area, then everything would be better." However, we are all ultimately responsible for what we are and what we become. Being rich or poor is an attitude.

— YOUR "HOPEOMETER" —

Each person is born with what I call a "hopeometer." No one knows what this mechanism looks like, but nevertheless it's there. Some people have allowed their hopeometers to rust out or suffer from neglect. Regardless of the condition of yours, I believe you can get it working again. Taking responsibility for your security is an inside job, and so is taking responsibility for your hope.

My mother was an expert "Hopeometer Repair Person." She kept her family together and gave us Christian values and principles by which to live. She kept her hopeometer going strong in the face of hard times. And she gave each of nine children a strong hopeometer to keep them going. Remember: Others can stop you temporarily, but you are the only one who can stop you permanently. As Winston Churchill said in his famous five-word speech, "Never, never, never give up!"

My mama had only a second grade education, but she still taught us the basic lessons of life. I didn't realize this until I became a high school principal and the newspaper came out with an article entitled, "Old-Fashioned Principal Teaches Old-Fashioned Principles." They quoted me as saying that Mama taught us some basic things: "Work hard, stay clean, love others, and go to church."

That's the culture in which I grew up. I never thought I would get out of Dixie. I thought I was doomed to stay there for the rest of my life. I assumed that someone would ask me to marry him, and I would have a bunch of kids and remain in my hometown. But I had one thing going for me. I had the dream of a better life. That was all I needed to keep my hopeometer activated.

I feel a need to tell my story because I think it will reactivate your hopeometer and give you fresh inspiration. When I speak, I often sense that many in my audiences did not start life the way I did. A lot of them, especially the younger ones, started life with more advantages. But regardless of your past, your future is a blank book. My prayer is that what you read here will help you fill those pages with hope and happiness. Please remember: I can, but more importantly, I believe you can too!

chapter 2

BEE
THERE

*T*he billion-dollar scandal, not only in our homes and the educational field but in business as well, is absenteeism.

I believe that if we take a job or responsibility, we must do every-thing in our power to fulfill that obligation. High school kids ask me how to get a raise. I tell them to go to work early and stay late. If you do more than you are paid to do, soon you are going to be paid more for what you do.

I'll never forget a fiery faculty meeting I attended when I was a teacher. I wanted to speak to the superintendent, so I got in line. Just in front of me was a veteran teacher who was about four feet tall. When her time came, she literally jumped at our superintendent, sticking her finger in his face. I'd never seen anyone talk to someone else in such a manner in ten years in the business world.

"You promised to have my room painted, and you promised that I would have no more than 125 students. I have 155 students, I only have 125 textbooks, and my room still needs to be painted! What are you going to do about it?" she demanded.

Mr. E. R. Cone, our superintendent, was a very wise man. He waited until the woman stopped talking, then he responded, "Honey, you took the job."

I agree. Whether our responsibilities are good, bad or indifferent, sometimes we have to suck it in and tough it out. Sometimes we cannot complain about how we feel or about our circumstances. We have to endure the situation. According to a Harvard University study, attitude is 85 per cent of the reason we get and keep jobs; skills are only 15 per cent. I thank God every day that my mother had the kind of attitude that kept her THERE *during our most trying times.*

On February 11, 1943, old Doc Smith came to see my mother. Mama was in the back of the house, working in the kitchen. It was two o'clock. There were nine of us children, so mealtime seemed a nonstop job. The six oldest children were still in school that day. My sister Martha Ann, age five, and my baby brother, Joseph, not yet two, were playing on the floor where Mama could keep an eye on them. I was there too. I was a month short of my fourth birthday.

The day was warm. Dixie, Georgia, is only ten miles north of the Florida border, so we seldom had extremely cold weather, much less snow. Aside from the wood stove for cooking in the kitchen, the only other source of heat in the house was a shallow fireplace in our small living room. I was nearly grown before I found out people with heated homes expected to stay warm on both sides at the same time.

Doc Smith owned an old Model A Ford that wheezed steam from the radiator and had loose fenders that rattled whenever it moved. Mama heard the doctor's noisy auto coming a hundred yards before it reached our house. She hastily wiped her hands on her faded apron, picked up little Joseph, and headed for the front door. "Come on, Martha Ann," she said. "You too, Mamie Claire. That's Doc Smith. I bet he's bringin' your daddy home, girls.

I Can. You Can Too!

Come on, now." We all hurried out to the porch.

Mama strained her eyes to catch a glimpse of Daddy. For the past year and a half, he had been feeling weak but had continued to go into the fields whenever possible. We were sharecroppers, and if we couldn't bring in a crop for the landlord, we got evicted.

Two weeks earlier, however, Daddy had collapsed, and Doc Smith had driven him six miles over to the hospital in Quitman. Tests revealed that Daddy had what was known back then as the "heart dropsy." Doc Smith felt that since Daddy was only forty-two and was now getting the best possible care, he'd probably recover in a couple of weeks.

Mama didn't go visit Daddy in the hospital because she didn't have anything respectable to wear. The only dress she owned was one she had made from a feed sack and some scrap cloth. Even on Sundays she would wait until everyone was in church and the sermon was started before she'd slip down to listen through an open window rather than go inside. Daddy was a deacon, and she didn't want to shame him in any way.

My sixteen-year-old sister, Voncille, had gone to see Daddy in the hospital. She had picked a handful of bright redbud flowers from our front yard and had hitched a ride to Quitman with a neighboring friend, Josie Harrell Bentley. She came back with a glowing report of how Daddy had loved the flowers and how he had been so happy to see her. We just knew it wouldn't be long before Daddy would be home again.

Before Doc Smith could even turn off the old Ford's motor, Mama was calling out to him. "Where's Mallory Darlington? I figured you to be carrying him home today, Doc."

Doc Smith opened the door and stepped down from the running board. He was wearing a starched shirt with sleeves rolled back two times. His tie, stiff collar, and dress coat were lying on the front seat of the car. One of his suspenders had come unclasped on the back of his pants, but he didn't seem to notice.

"Afternoon, Miss Bertha. This old car and I both could use some cold water if you've got some." Doc walked wide of the steaming radiator cap as he rounded the front of the car. Mama waved him inside and led the way.

"I just drew a bucket from the well a little while before you came," said Mama from the kitchen. "Come back here and help yourself."

Doc Smith surveyed our house as he passed through the two rooms leading to the kitchen. The living room had two crates for chairs, an old sofa glider, and some spike nails pounded into the wall to hang coats on. Two small side bedrooms were cramped with two beds each. One room had a "potty chair" pot in the corner. In the middle room stood a used ice box crate that my eighteen-year-old brother, Richard, had hauled from town. It now served as an indoor closet for us. The kitchen had one unvarnished and battered old oak table in the middle of the room where we all gathered for our meals. Around it were two broken chairs and some crates with boards stretched between them like bleacher seats.

The kitchen had one small shelf above the cook stove. On the floor all around the walls in every room were jars of butter beans, tomatoes, peas, okra, string beans, jams, and jellies that Mama and the older girls had canned during the summer. "We've got good neighbors," Mama said, pointing to the canned vegetables. "Last year when most of them finished picking their crops, they told us we could glean the fields for whatever was left. My children worked hard. We did all right at that."

Doc Smith smiled in agreement, then dipped himself a ladle of water from the kitchen pail.

"You see Mallory today?" Mama asked.

Doc slowly replaced the ladle on the nail on the wall. He pulled a wrinkled handkerchief from his back pocket and wiped his mouth. "Sit down here a minute with me, Bertha," said Doc. "I need to talk to you about Mallory."

"If it's about the money, I want you to know that we aim to do something about that," said Mama. "Richard's got himself a lead on a part-time job at the cotton mill, and, uh, Voncille, she's able to work after school."

"It's not the money —"

"And once spring comes we'll all be able to get jobs tilling and planting, and we'll put in a garden of our own, and —"

"Mallory passed away this morning, Miss Bertha."

"— and my girls can clean house for people, and my boys can run errands and —"

"He's gone, Mrs. Darlington. Mallory's dead."

"— and we can plant or till or do a garden or can vegetables or make food for shut-ins or —"

Doc reached over and grabbed Mama's wrists. "Stop it, Bertha. He's dead. We did all we could for him, but his heart just gave out. Lord knows, I don't want to face it any more than you do. But it's a fact. He's gone. Mallory Darlington is dead."

— FACING THE FUTURE —

My father didn't look old enough to be in a casket. His hair was coal black, his skin was still tan from summer, and his six-foot, two-inch frame was lean and muscular. Only the callused hands and broken fingernails offered evidence of a man overworked, overworried, and underpaid.

Mama couldn't control her grief. She was so emotionally distraught, she became physically ill and was bedridden. Her worries were justified. With only a second-grade education and no work experience, she qualified for no jobs. She had nine children to feed and clothe somehow. Worst of all, she had been told either to buy the house she was living in or vacate the premises at the end of the season. Not knowing what to do, my mother yielded to anxiety and became an emotional invalid.

In the next few days, however, Mama taught me one of the most important lessons I have ever learned. It's a lesson that applies to all areas of life — career, family, social, mental, physical — all areas! My mother made a conscious decision to *be there* for her family. What choices did she have? The same ones you and I face every day of our lives. She could have stayed in bed and given up. No one would have blamed her. With her lack of education and the obstacles she faced in raising nine children, many people would have given up. Every day we read about mothers and fathers who walk away from difficult family situations. But my mother made the decision to *be there*, and her decision has had a dramatic impact on my life.

How many times have you awakened in the morning and wanted to go back to sleep? How often do the pressures of your career make getting up and going to work seem unbearable? So many times in my career in the business world, and later as an educator, I was ready to quit! The chances are good that you've felt the same way too, on more than one occasion. However, sometimes the best work is done by people who don't *want* to do what they have to do but who are nonetheless courageous enough to get up and get going! Who are the successful people? They are the ones who do the things that unsuccessful people refuse to do.

The parent who "hangs in there" during the teenage years, the manager who goes the extra mile for an employee, the teacher who comes back to the classroom when everything seems hopeless — these are the successful people in life who, like my mother, are making the choice to *be there*.

We expected our relatives to come to our aid. It was traditional for family to stick together in times of trouble. But when our family members explained to us the kind of help they wanted to give, we weren't at all happy. "The plan is simple, Bertha," one cousin told Mama. "We'll take the oldest young'uns and divide them among the families and use them as field workers. We'll take your three little ones and put them in the county home."

"Orphanage? *Orphanage?*" Mama stammered. "My babies? Split up my family? No! No sir, never! You'll do that over my dead body!"

"Well," said the cousin, "Mallory *is* dead, Bertha, and the way you look, now...."

Mama pulled herself up in bed. "I ain't dead!" she announced defiantly. "And you're about to see that Mallory's memory ain't dead, either. Get out of my way!"

Mama pulled back the covers and stood up. "Children!" she yelled. "Come here. Every one of you. We've got some talking to do."

— AIN'T NOBODY GOING NO PLACE —

A family council was held in our kitchen that night. Mama stood at the far end of the table, while we children sat watching her. The chair at the head of the table — Daddy's chair — remained empty and unmoved. If Daddy wasn't there physically that night, he certainly was spiritually. In an odd way, we were missing him, yet feeling his presence. We were Daddy's family, and as long as we stuck together, we felt that he would be with us.

"I know y'all are grievin' about your daddy and you don't feel like doing anything but pulling the bedcovers over your head and hiding," said Mama. "I'd like to do that too. But we just can't."

"Is Martha Ann and the babies going to the county home, Mama?" asked my eleven-year-old sister, June Ernestine. "I heard the neighbors say they was."

"What about me, Mama?" asked nine-year-old Douglas. "Do I really have to go sharecropping tobacco upstate with our cousins?"

Mama raised her hands for silence. "Ain't nobody going no place," said Mama. "We're a family, and if we work as a family, we'll pull through this. But everybody's got to do a part. The work is going to be hard on us, but at least we'll be together."

"I'll work, Mama," said little Martha Ann. "I'm a good worker. And I don't even go to school yet."

Mama smiled. "*All* my babies are good workers. I know you'll all help out."

"We staying here, Mama?" asked ten-year-old Mary Lou. "Is this still going to be our house?"

Mama shook her head. "I talked to a woman in town today. She's willing to give us a chance at buying a $400 home she has vacant. If we can pay ten dollars a month, she'll sell us the house and one acre of ground. That'll give us a place to stay and a spot for a garden. I talked to the preacher too. He said he would announce it next Sunday that we need some food and clothes to help us through until spring planting comes."

The children all looked puzzled. "But...ain't that charity, Mama?" my sister Evelyn asked slowly. "Daddy said we was workers. He said we don't need no charity."

Mama's eyes narrowed, and for an instant they flashed anger. Just as quickly, however, the reaction passed. She calmed herself, cleared her throat, and then spoke evenly. "Now, listen to me, children. Your daddy did all he could to provide us a good living. And while he was alive, I followed him in whatever he said to do. We started sharecropping in Millen, Georgia, before any of y'all was born. Whenever Daddy said we needed to move, we moved. I never gave him any argument, 'cause I figured he knew what was best for us. We moved five times and I never said a word."

"Things are different now, though. Daddy's gone home to his reward, and I'm the one in charge. I've got to do whatever's necessary to help us survive. And y'all have got to trust me the same way we always trusted Daddy. So, if the church folks can give us a little help, then we're going to accept it. The preacher showed me where the Bible says, 'Let the elders take care of the widows and their children.' It ain't shameful accepting help from the church."

"Daddy used to cut wood for the old widow up on the hard road, right, Mama?" said Douglas. "He didn't take money for it, neither."

"Sure, he helped folks," said Mama. "Your daddy helped lots of folks. He taught a Sunday school lesson on Sunday and then lived it the rest of the week. Your daddy has friends who would love to repay him for his kindnesses. They'll help us now. You watch and see. There's good folks around here. Lots of good folks."

"But how are we gonna get *ten dollars* every month to pay the landlord?" asked Voncille. "That's more money than I've ever seen in my life. Used to, the landlord would take the crops we raised and then pay us some money. Now, we can't work the land, and we're supposed to pay a new landlord some money. How we gonna do that, Mama?"

Mama lowered her head a moment and then cast her eyes sideways to where Richard was sitting. Richard flashed a reassuring grin at Mama, then nodded for her to explain.

"Richard's taken a job at the cotton mill," said Mama. "He starts next week. It breaks my heart to see my firstborn get just three months from graduating high school and not be able to finish, but he's the only one I can turn to. Either Richard takes a job or it's the county home for Martha Ann, Mamie Claire, and little Joseph. Richard don't want that any more than I do. He's a good boy, your brother Richard."

"Thank you, Richard," the little voices around the table echoed each other. "Thank you. We love you."

Richard's face grew flushed. He lowered his head, and at once he was both embarrassed to be referred to as the man in the family and very pleased to be the key person making it possible for the family to stay together.

"Shucks, I don't mind," was all he said. The look on Richard's face was as though all his life he had wanted to do something significant, and now he'd been given that chance. At age twelve, Richard had rheumatic fever and his heart was impaired. As a result, he'd never been able to do the heavy manual labor the other men and boys in our area did. Now, he looked strong. He had a sense of purpose and mission in life. Mama had leaned on him, and he held her up. He was, indeed, a man, a strong man.

From a career perspective, Richard's decision to *be there* was a difficult one. It would have been very easy for him to do what was best for him personally — and our family could have suffered tragically.

Many years later, when I was managing employees in the business world of real estate and later direct sales, I told my co-workers and employees about Richard's sacrifice and encouraged them to sacrifice "short-term" pain for "long-term" gain. Many who grudgingly took this direction were grateful years later. One man who wanted to leave our company for a "greener-grass" situation was particularly moved by Richard's story and made the decision to *be there* (stay with us). Ninety days later the organization that had recruited him so heavily collapsed.

I can't guess God's plan for anyone, but I do know this about Richard. From that day forward, he looked life square in the eye and showed greater bravery than anyone I've ever known. As an adult, when Richard's heart was growing weaker with each passing day, he moved to Texas and volunteered to let Dr. Michael DeBakey and Dr. Denton Cooley do experimental heart surgery on him. Richard became famous. His picture was in *Life* magazine, and his name was in all the newspapers. People came to show the pictures to Mama and to brag about her brave son, but Mama only smiled and nodded. *Life* magazine couldn't tell her anything new about her boy's bravery. She'd known all about his courage ever since the family council in our kitchen in February of 1943 when, as an eighteen-year-old boy, he rose to meet our family's need and became a man.

And so the Darlingtons became a family of both love and discipline. Mama's rules were basic and functional: "Work hard. Stay clean. Love others. And go to church."

— KEEPING LIFE IN PERSPECTIVE —

Growing up in Dixie, Georgia, as a poor child had its challenges, but nothing that seemed too exceptional when I looked at the way most other folks lived back then. I was brought up in a culture where people went to the bathroom on the outside and cooked on the inside. Nowadays, it's popular to cook on the outside and go to the bathroom on the inside.

I was not raised *poor*, I was raised *pore*. Do you know the difference between poor and pore? When I once tried to tell my mother-in-law how pore I was raised, she said, "Honey, so what? We all grew up poor." But you see, being poor is when everyone around is poor and they have the same standard of living, not knowing that there's anything better. Being pore is when folks up on the hard road have a lot more than you do, and you know it. Do you know what a "hard road" is? It's a paved road. Being pore is when the poor folks up on the hard road have all indoor plumbing and you still have a path leading to an outhouse.

Mama never had it easy those early years, but she always had an internal contentment and a wonderful perspective on life. She had come close to losing her home and children; yet, when she made the decision to *be there*, she escaped that near tragedy. Those difficult circumstances made her fully realize that since the most important things in life were God, her children, and her house, and since she still had those things, nothing else really mattered a great deal. Life really was pretty good.

Perhaps you've heard of the patient who was told he had cancer and would be dead in six months. Later, the doctor called the man and apologized profusely because the reports had accidentally been switched and there was really nothing wrong with the man. At that moment, the man looked at a stack of unpaid bills on his desk and threw them up in the air, laughing out loud. Who cared about the bills — he *wasn't* going to die. Hooray! Life's great! Everything comes down to perspective.

Mama kept her perspective. She was born in 1905 and lived until 1979, and never once did she look back on those early years and refer to them as hard times. She maintained a hopeometer in her heart that constantly made her feel that life today is good and tomorrow can only get better.

And you know what? Life did get better. With the exception of Richard, who sacrificed for all of us, all of Mama's children graduated from high school. Several graduated from college. Richard became nationally known for his help with heart research. Martha Ann became an outstanding school teacher, married a preacher, and spent three terms as a missionary in Africa. Evelyn raised five children and became a well-respected nurse. Douglas has had an excellent career with the Nabisco Company. The other sisters — Mary Lou, June, and Voncille (the oldest daughter, who shouldered much of the "motherly" burdens during those early years) — have become wonderful wives and mothers. My own career has been very diversified: school teacher, high school principal, real estate manager, direct sales manager, wife, mother of three, speaker, and author. My work now, as the "I CAN Lady," is the most fulfilling and challenging career I can imagine.

Yes, my mother was quite a lady. When I was in the eleventh grade, all the children, including my brothers-in-law, tore down the old house and built a new home for Mama, Joseph, and me on the same plot of ground. People loved Mama. When my brothers-in-law were dating my sisters, they used to say, "Come on, Mrs. Darlington, and go to the fair with us." They took her to the movies and school basketball games and wherever else they were going. Mama was full of life. She was richer in spirit than a lot of millionaires I've met in my life.

Mama never took a college course in accounting, but she always managed to meet her mortgage payments. She never attended a home economics class, but she reared nine children who became fine citizens and good parents.

Life can teach you things if you're willing to learn. Mama learned all she needed to know about goal-setting that day she had to decide how to keep her family together. She learned all she needed to know about public oratory that day she stood before us and explained what needed to be done in order for us to survive.

In my life, I've learned a lot of things. Some things I learned the hard way by making mistakes, falling on my face, losing money, and embarrassing myself. Other things I learned the more intelligent way by reading books, listening to cassettes, attending classes, and seeking advice from people smarter than me. Yes, I've learned a lot of lessons, but in all this time, no lesson has proved more valuable, more truthful, or more universal in application than the lesson

Mama taught me by the way she lived: *It's not where you start, it's where you finish that counts.*

— WHAT ABOUT YOU? —

I have shared my own "start," because life once seemed hopeless to me. While I'm not "finished" yet, I have accomplished more than most people expected. And because of the lessons my mother taught me, I *know* the best is yet to come.

The same thing applies to you. No matter where you're starting from today, you can finish the way you want. You may have *everything* going your way — or you may have lost a loved one, been terminated from your job, gone through a traumatic divorce, had a tremendous financial reversal, or experienced any number of terrible events. No matter how bleak things may seem

HEARTITUDE:

It's not where you start,

it's where you finish

that counts.

♡

or how impossible a situation may appear, you need to realize that you always have options. Maybe they won't be pleasant. To keep our family together, my Mama had to leave the farm and my brother had to quit high school and work in the cotton mill. But whether bleak or rough or challenging or scary, you *always* have options. You can exercise those options to your advantage. You can succeed! No one thought Mamie Claire Darlington of Dixie, Georgia, would be able to succeed, but "I can and you can too!" And it all starts with a decision to "bee there."

— I CAN...AND *HERE'S HOW* YOU CAN TOO! —

1. "Bee There." Bloom where you're planted. Have the courage to persevere in the face of adversity.

2. Discover *your* mission and purpose in life. Remember that once Richard found his "cause," he increased his self-confidence and motivation.

3. Become a person of love and discipline. "Work hard. Stay clean. Love others. And go to church." These are still words to grow by.

4. Remember that your *perspective* makes the difference in life. The way you look at life is your reality. My mother could have looked at what she didn't have and given up. Instead, she looked at what she did have, and life got better every day.

5. Look for the lessons in life, and be willing to learn. Our victories *and* our mistakes are either stepping stones or stumbling blocks. You determine which by your willingness to learn.

chapter 3

BEE
YOURSELF

*M*y good friend Dr. Tom
McDougal is not only an
excellent dentist but an excellent
speaker as well. Tom discusses the
"how to's" of developing an
outstanding practice with other dentists. He is probably the best
in his field. Tom is an inspirational role model for all of us in
that he has the physical, mental, and spiritual areas of his life
in balance. But he would be the first to tell you that he has to
work at keeping the balance.

Recently, while having my teeth cleaned, I was giving Tom the
rundown on my schedule, and he expressed some surprise.
"Mamie," he asked, "when do you relax?"

I jokingly replied that relaxation was not on my "To Do" list.

Tom didn't laugh. He went into his private office and came
out a few minutes later with a book, **When I Relax I Feel
Guilty,** by Tim Hansel.* With great insight, love, and the
proper dose of "Let-me-tell-you-from-my-experience," Tom
said to me, "Mamie, one of the reasons you work so hard is for
other people — to please them. This is one of your greatest
strengths.

However, a strength taken too far becomes a weakness. You

34

must do something for yourself as well as for others. You must not be overly concerned about what others think of you! You must be yourself!"

Dr. McDougal sure pegged me right. One of my greatest concerns was what others thought. I sure didn't want anyone saying Mamie McCullough wasn't a hard worker. I'd show 'em. I would work so hard.... But Tom helped me see that I had to be myself. Now I work hard when I know I need to work hard, and I relax when I need to relax. I'm not completely out of the woods, but I'm making progress in this area.

You must not compare yourself to others. Instead, be the best you that you can be. "Bee yourself!"

Folks are old-fashioned in Dixie, Georgia. They believe a woman should graduate from high school, get married, and *then* have children. I still believe that way. Nowadays, however, some people are getting it backward. They're having their children and then considering the possibility of marriage. But during the 1950s in Dixie, folks thought that a woman should want nothing more than a home with a husband and children. That's what "being yourself" was supposed to mean to me.

I graduated from Dixie High School with twenty-two other students. I have forty-eight nieces and nephews, and so between my eight brothers and sisters, we had a lot of babies. No one expected us to attend college or to do anything different with our lives. But I wanted something different.

For many reasons — some good, some bad — I felt I was different. I had a bigger vision than Dixie, Georgia, had given me. I knew

*Tim Hansel, *When I Relax I Feel Guilty* (Elgin, IL: David C. Cook, 1979).

I wanted to become a better person, but I didn't know how. I knew that people with more education were the ones who got the good jobs, so I knew I wanted more education. But I don't remember many people saying to me, "Mamie Claire, why don't you go to college? Why don't you become a teacher? a secretary? a counselor?" Very few people ever said to me, "I believe in you, and I believe you can make it." Instead, I developed a very poor self-image that I have had to work to overcome all my life and that has been a serious obstacle to my success.

— LIFE IN DIXIE —

My perception of the world was basically what I observed in Dixie. I had some fun, don't misunderstand me. As a ninth grader I was five feet nine, so I played on the girls' basketball team for four years. We won the league championship in 1957, and somewhere today there's a trophy in a dusty storeroom with my name on it.

I went through Dixie school with some wonderful people. I have a special friend, Elizabeth Jones Simpson, who has been my friend since the first grade. She's still living in Dixie. Elizabeth was the one I wanted to be like — she and my sister Martha Ann. Elizabeth lived up on the hard road and had a beautiful mother and father. I thought they were the richest people I had ever known. Elizabeth's mother, Miss Harriet Jones, and her father, Mr. Carl Winter Jones, were the epitome of a southern lady and gentleman — always courteous, kind, caring, and loving.

The Joneses were very kind to me and encouraged and helped me in so many ways. They were one of the especially positive influences in my early life. I remember once when I was seven, Miss Harriet took me to Lucille's Beauty Shop in Dixie and had a permanent put in my hair. I thought that was just wonderful! I will always be grateful to both of them, and to Elizabeth and her sister, Jenny, for allowing me to be a part of their family in those early years.

I had no time for hobbies or school clubs. All during high school I held after-school, weekend, and summer jobs in nearby Quitman, at a dime store and a clothing store, or else I worked in the tobacco fields. I had one steady boyfriend, good ol' Willard, but Mama only let me go to church with him on Sundays and have one other date per week from time to time. Even then, she preferred that I double-date with my sister Martha Ann.

I was proposed to by Willard, but Mama wanted me to finish high school. We decided not to talk about weddings until then. Mama believed a high school education was important. She recognized her lack of education and the difficulties having only a second-grade education caused her, so I always tried to do well in school, if for no other reason than to please her.

Speaking honestly, I was probably no better than an average student. I hated mathematics and consequently made poor grades in most math classes. I was an A student in home economics, however, because learning how to sew, cook, clean house, and feed a baby made sense to me. After all, that's what everyone expected me to spend the rest of my life doing. Mrs. Hatcher, my teacher, used to praise me for my work and encourage me to enter my projects in fairs and school competitions.

Now, don't misunderstand. I believe one of life's noblest callings is that of wife and mother. In my opinion, it's terribly unfair to criticize anyone who has chosen to express herself in that manner. And my challenge to *be yourself*, when answered in this way, is answered wonderfully. I also believe that those who choose to express themselves in a career outside the home should not be criticized. For some, the call to be yourself means a combination of home and outside activities.

Here's my point: Be yourself, not what others say you should be, but what you see as your calling in life. Sure you get insight from others. You might even take some psychological testing to discover your strengths and weaknesses. However, in the final analysis, you must accept the responsibility and make the decision to *be yourself.*

— CHILDHOOD MEMORIES —

When I think back on my childhood education, three things stand out. The first is that I always admired and respected my school teachers. Those ladies were always so clean and attractive, so intelligent and composed, so graceful and wise. Mrs. Wade, in the fourth grade, loved us and made us feel as though we were special people. Mrs. Moffett, my fifth-grade teacher, was a strong disciplinarian, but a great one to praise and encourage us. I loved them all.

Today, people will occasionally ask me, "Mamie, why do you always say yes whenever a group of teachers asks you to speak?" My answer is simple: I've always had a special feeling in my heart for educators. I've got debts of gratitude to repay to some teachers who spent time with me when I was young. While I can never directly repay those teachers, I can give others what those wonderful people gave me. This sharing with others is the finest form of repayment, because it allows the kindness of those dedicated teachers to live forever. *Those who affect children will affect generations to come.*

I do look back fondly to those early years in the classroom. But while some teachers were kind and encouraging to me, others (perhaps inadvertently) were judgmental. That is my second memory of my education and, unfortunately, a negative one.

You see, when I was a child (and it still happens today), a youngster became "labeled" early in life. Those labels stuck with you all through school and put you into a slot that society felt you merited, making it extremely difficult to be yourself. I, for instance, was labeled "one of those poor Darlington kids." I had no father, my mother was uneducated, and my oldest brother had quit school to go to work in the mill. *Obviously*, Mamie Claire was only fit for "birthin' young'uns and cannin' tomatoes."

This was truly a shame, for had it not been for a quirk of good timing combined with the intervention of some Christian aid, I indeed would have become the very sort of person most others expected me to be.

I was fortunate to outdistance my label. But I often wonder about the others who weren't as lucky. How many potential Einsteins and Rembrandts and Sally Rides and Barbara Jordans and Bill Cosbys did we miss because someone labeled them "farm hand," "factory worker," or "waitress" early in life?

Labeling is dangerous. If we begin to classify anyone as a bully or a class clown or a dummy or a wallflower, in time he or she will become convinced that that is his or her real identity. *As you imagine yourself to be, so in time you will become.* Used in a positive way, this can be a wonderful motivation. Used negatively, it can stifle a person's entire potential — a frightening thought. As I often say when I speak: "As we see people, we treat them; as we treat them, oftentimes they become." As parents, educators, and business leaders, we need to be more concerned about "I cans" than "IQ's."

— CHILD ABUSE AND SELF ESTEEM —

My third memory is the most tragic and traumatic memory any young person can have. I was abused as a child. Until my mother died in 1979, I never told the story, even though the incidences occurred when I was five to ten years old. It took me many more years to gather the courage to relive the horrible memories of the abuse and to discuss the facts with audiences as I speak all over the US, Canada, and Mexico. When I learned that the horror of child abuse was so widespread, however, I knew I must tell how this affected my life.

Child abuse is the most misunderstood reality in our society. This horror doesn't always mean rape. Exposure of private parts and "touching" is very common among the sick individuals who brutalize and terrorize children. Child abusers can't be identified by their social standing or financial resources. Abuse involves young and old, rich and poor, and crosses every socioeconomic spectrum of our society. Parents who are confident they are protecting their children should be aware that this protection is not always as easy as it might seem.

HEARTITUDE:

Those who affect children

will affect generations

to come.

♡

I was fortunate never to have been raped. However, this doesn't minimize the devastation I felt from having to see men expose themselves to me or having myself touched and made to feel "dirty." There were men from church as well as men who didn't attend church who managed to manipulate me into uncomfortable situations that a child has no way of avoiding.

What would you think about your child's walking a short distance to the church to practice piano? Would you suspect an "upstanding" man in the community who "innocently" sat on the piano bench to listen was fondling your child? My family didn't suspect. What would a very small child do who was invited to come into the back yard and see the baby chickens or new puppies? Would you suspect the child saw more than she expected or wanted to see?

How would you feel about your child's sitting in a relative's lap and reading the "funny papers," being "groped" behind the newspaper, while no one even suspected? What is a child supposed to think when she's raised in an era when respecting adults, doing what you are told to do, and never questioning authority are valued as highly as it was in the early 1940s?

HEARTITUDE:

As you imagine yourself to be, so in time you will become.

♡

My family never suspected, and, frankly, if these situations hadn't occurred in my own life, I probably wouldn't be suspicious, either. My objective in mentioning these terribly painful situations is to help others be less naive and to help some other child avoid the emotional pain and scars that accompany these damaging scenarios.

After my horrible experiences, I held my head low. I didn't talk. I didn't answer any questions. I felt dirty and sinful and ugly.

I hated the people involved, and I hated myself too. I was now a "bad girl." I knew that for sure. Only bad girls got involved in nasty things like that. I wanted to forget the whole thing, but that was impossible. The images of what happened haunted my memory. I didn't want to be myself. I wanted to be anybody *but* me. How can you be yourself with that kind of shame and guilt in your mind?

It never occurred to me to tell anyone. Mama and my sisters wouldn't be able to stand up against that kind of meanness. They might get hurt too! My father was dead, and my oldest brother was working long, hard hours in another town. *I felt there was no one there to take up for me.*

All sorts of wild imaginings went through my head about what happened to bad little girls if they were found out. Would my family disown me? Would I be sent to reform school or the county home? Would I go to jail?

I lived in terror both day and night. When I went to sleep, I often had nightmares. During the day, I stayed close to my sisters. On the outside I could smile and feign contentment, but inwardly I had no confidence and no personal satisfaction about who I was. It took me years to overcome the impact of child abuse on my already negative self-image.

As I began to slowly work through the difficult process of "replacing" horror with hope and helplessness with healing, I realized that despite how difficult it would be for me personally to "relive" these childhood experiences, I had to offer encouragement to those "walking wounded" who, through no fault of their own, have walked in these painful shoes.

For these reasons I am writing: *I Wish I Had Someone To Take Up*

For Me, Help For Those Who Need Hope And Healing. This book looks at the many different types of abuse so prevalent in our society, contains many of the details of my own experiences, looks at ways to prevent abuse, and discusses how to get on with the abundant life we have all been promised. According to research, more than 50 percent of all females have experienced some form of sexual abuse. Recent FBI reports say the figure may be as high as 80 percent.

I am a fanatic regarding the necessity of protecting our children and teaching them how to avoid circumstances in which they might encounter abuse. I stress this to parents, teachers, and civic leaders. Prevention simply cannot be emphasized too much.

Child abuse isn't something new, of course; it's just a topic that has recently gained more public attention. This attention has resulted in some positive changes in our ways of dealing with the problem. We now have 24-hour police "hot lines" open to handle reports of child abuse. There are state and federal laws that now require nurses and doctors to report all cases of suspected child abuse. We also have locally- and nationally-funded programs that provide family shelters, caseworker assistance, and psychological counseling for victims of child abuse.

I laud all these marvelous innovations for dealing with this disastrous situation. Nevertheless, I caution all parents and teachers not to be lulled into a state of complacency. We must remember that the first priority is to do all we can to protect our children from ever becoming victims in the first place.

Child abuse is a crime. Equally as bad, it is a moral, social, and psychological offense. The incidents I endured as a small child made me feel unworthy of people's love and respect. They added to my shyness and lack of confidence. They made me examine myself frequently in the mirror of my mind, and turn away filled with self-loathing and personal disrespect.

No one, but *no one*, should be allowed to do that to *any* child.

— CHANGING MY IMAGE —

In addition to all the other things working against my feeling free to be myself, I hated my appearance. I didn't like my height, I didn't like my teeth, I didn't like my nose, and I didn't like my hair. Physically and emotionally, I had never accepted myself.

Now, you may be thinking that all kids go through a stage when they look gangly, lose their baby teeth, and stay dirty. But I never grew out of that stage inwardly. In my mind, I was ugly my entire childhood. And what made my feelings worse was that my sister, Martha Ann, was so beautiful.

Nobody ever called me ugly or homely. They would just see me and my sister coming and say, "Oh look, it's that pretty little Martha Ann — and, uh, Mamie Claire." That was my identity in life. I was pretty Martha Ann's sister, "ol' what's-her-name." As I look back, I feel sorry for those people in Dixie, because they never knew exactly what to say to me. But at the time, I only felt sorry for myself.

Martha had a perfect, five-feet-six-inch curvaceous body. Her teeth were straight, her hair was bouncy and full, and her features were classic. Not me. By fifth grade I was a towering five feet nine inches. I wasn't just skinny; I was scrawny. The only way people could tell my front from my back was by the way my feet were pointing. If we had tried out for parts in the school production of *The Wizard of Oz*, Martha would have been cast as Dorothy, and

I would have been the Scarecrow.

By age ten, I picked up the nickname "Happy Child." This isn't as positive as it sounds. People called me "Happy Child" because my front teeth were so bucked and protruding, not because of my pleasant disposition. If you cannot get your lip down over your teeth, you smile a lot. Even when I would cry, I would still have this stupid smile on my face. Now, if you happen to see me in person or if you look at my picture on the jacket of this book, you'll know that my teeth have become pretty and straight.

They're *my* teeth. I say they're mine because I bought and paid for them. After a good dentist's bridgework, people now think of me as happy because of my disposition, not my teeth.

My hair was also terrible, sticking out in every direction, frizzy in back, flat in front, and springy on the sides. Martha and I used to roll our hair on rags on Saturday night. On Sunday before church we would let it down. Martha's would come out fluffy and soft and curly, while I waited in terror for someone to ask me when I was going to take mine down. Often, it would look as if I had stuck my finger in a light socket.

— FALSE COMPARISONS —

I felt Martha Ann had everything I didn't have. The fact that this wasn't true didn't occur to me at the time. I blamed all my problems on her. The truth was that I had a very poor self-image and chose to make her my scapegoat.

One cause of a poor self-image is comparing ourselves with others, as I did with Martha Ann. But the biggest competitor you should have in life is yourself. Who are you in competition with? My self-imposed competition was with Martha and her average height, her beautiful skin and hair, and her straight teeth. How could anyone tall and skinny with red welts and frizzy hair compare positively to Martha?

Many years later, I learned a very important lesson. Success is not measured by how we compare with others. Success is measured by comparing our accomplishments to our capabilities. Strive to be the very best "you" that you can become. Rather than going for the world's record in your first attempt, go for a personal record. If you keep setting personal records long enough, one day you may challenge the world's record.

> **HEARTITUDE:**
>
> *As we see people,*
>
> *we treat them,*
>
> *and as we treat them,*
>
> *often they become.*
>
> ♡

One woman compared her worst features to someone else's best features, and by age 38 she was a scrub woman living on welfare. Then she read Claude M. Bristol's *The Magic of Believing*.* She started believing and looking at her positive qualities, one of which was the ability to make people laugh. Since that time, even though she still doesn't compete with the beauties of the world, Phyllis Diller has earned as much as $1,000,000 in a single year. She took her own best features and talents and made the most of them.

— A MATURE SELF-IMAGE —

What's a good self-image? It isn't an egotistical "I'm-greater-than-you" or "I'm-better-than-you" attitude. Some people confuse a healthy self-image with conceit. This is *not* what I'm

*Claude M. Bristol, *The Magic of Believing* (New York: Pocket Books, 1983).

talking about. As Zig Ziglar says, "Conceit is a weird disease that makes everybody sick...except the one that's got it!" A healthy self-image is simply becoming the best you that you can possibly be. If you get up in the morning, look in the mirror, and see a nobody, you feel you're hopeless and have nothing to offer. Often, you don't try your best because you don't feel you deserve the good things in life: a good marriage, beautiful and healthy children, a steady job, a spacious home, or a nice car.

Remember: *No* one can make you feel inferior without your permission! Are you giving other people permission to make you feel like a second-class person? I was guilty of feeling like a "0" on a scale of 1-10 for so many years. Then I read Zig Ziglar's book, *See You At The Top**, and learned I could be a 10. During the last 20 years I have been writing about and teaching the I CAN Way of Life. While working to help others, I have discovered that I don't have to feel second class because of the things that happened to me many years ago.

Some of the features I saw as flaws I could change, like my teeth and my nose. Since I hadn't had braces as a child, I decided to have my teeth molded and capped evenly with bridgework.

My college roommate gave me an idea for fixing my nose.

One day she remarked, "I'm going to get my nose fixed when I graduate."

I asked her, "Terri, what's wrong with your nose?"

"It's too big," she answered.

"Oh, am I ever in luck," I replied. "Mine's too small. I want what you take off." (Made sense to me!)

*Zig Ziglar, *See You at the Top* (New York: Pelican, 1984).

I Can. You Can Too!

We both laughed at my joke, but I was serious enough to read Dr. Maxwell Maltz's phenomenal book *Psycho-Cybernetics** and afterward consult with three plastic surgeons about having my nose fixed. Back in the '60s, plastic surgery was not as popular as it is today. I told only my closest friends that I was coming to Dallas to get a bigger nose. Why three surgeons? Even a car repair requires three estimates, so I took the Yellow Pages and got appointments for three estimates.

One surgeon told me that he could surgically remove a small rib from my side, cut it into even smaller pieces, and use one of the pieces to form a graft to the cartilage in my nose. This would help extend my nose and flair my nostrils. I would finally breathe with ease and no longer gasp when I was frustrated. He extended my nose by one-eighth of an inch, and the results were marvelous. No more hyperventilation, no more red welts, and in the mirror of my mind I saw my face as normal.

By the way, if you ever see me scratch my nose and giggle, you'll now understand why! (If you don't "get it," go back and reread the last two paragraphs.)

When people ask me how old I am, I say, "I don't know. I don't count the three years I was pregnant or the two years I was sick." However, I am definitely at the age where if it doesn't hurt it doesn't work. There are days when I wake up and start to get out of bed, and one leg says, "No, I'm not coming."

When I turned forty (I forget exactly when that was), I started gaining weight. I had heard of being fat, forty, and downhill. I thought, *How can I teach people to believe in themselves and be forty and downhill?* It seems that after forty, things either turn gray,

*Maxwell Maltz, *Psycho-Cybernetics* (New York: Pocket Books, 1983).

flatten out, or turn loose. Well, I refused to let anyone call me a gray-headed lady. My hair was only faded until I got smart and shaded it. I was a young lady with old hair. Now I am a young lady with young-looking hair. I have gone from "faded" to "shaded!" I've learned it isn't the *downhill* that counts, it's the *upkeep* — both mentally and physically.

— I CAN SAY NO —

Another important part of being yourself is learning to say no. I'm a person who enjoys pleasing others. Nothing makes me happier than bringing joy into others' lives. When I can do something that brings a smile to the face of my children or friends, I'm in "hog-heaven." However, I've learned that many times our weaknesses are extensions of our strengths.

HEARTITUDE:

No one can make you

feel inferior

without your

permission.

♡

If one of my strengths is pleasing people, but I go to the extreme to please others, like taking too many speaking engagements in too few days and becoming worn out before the presentation, I have really hurt everyone involved: the client, my family, myself, as well as the quality of the presentation. In other words, nobody wins unless I learn to say no.

People with a healthy self-image learn to say no at the proper time.

I Can. You Can Too!

You may be like me and have to learn to listen to an objective third party for input as you develop the strength to say no, and I strongly encourage you to do so if that's your situation.

Developing a healthy self-image is vitally important to the success each of us seeks. Children with healthy self-esteem like themselves and don't want to be someone else. Therefore, those with a high level of personal belief in self are more prepared to say no to peer pressure that would encourage them to *be someone else*. For the same reason, they find it easier to say no to chemicals that would alter their perceptions of themselves.

Business men and women who learn to say no avoid the peer pressure to "stay out late with the guys" or "have dinner with an office companion" and risk having these situations cause serious problems at home.

I believe a healthy self-image is the foundation stone upon which we must all build our success. Please remember that almost everyone has moments of self-doubt. I read recently, "We teach most what we most need to learn." There are still times when my childhood traumas and self-doubts sneak into my mind. If this happens to you, *fight back*. Don't allow those concepts to pervade your thoughts and actions. Instead, fill your mind with the good, clean, pure, powerful, and positive — good books, good cassette tapes, good seminars, supporting and loving friends — anything and everything *good* to displace the negative. Faith and fear cannot exist together. Be yourself — your best self, but *yourself.*

— I CAN...AND *HERE'S HOW* YOU CAN TOO! —

1. "Bee Yourself." If you work to be the best you can be, not by comparison with others but through personal growth; if you work to "fix" those areas of your self-concept that are "fixable" (education, physical appearance, etc.); if you learn to say no to those who would encourage you to fail; and if you fill your mind with the good, clean, pure, powerful, and positive — then you're truly becoming all you can be.

2. Beware of negative labeling. Never tease in a hurting way. Remember: "Sticks and stones may break my bones, but words can break my heart." Point out the good you see in others. Be a "people builder" not a one-person "people demolition crew."

3. Take a stand on child abuse in your community. Have the courage to be solution-conscious and to work toward prevention. Please be available to listen to children, and for their sake take action to help them! Make sure the appropriate people (victims, perpetrators, community leaders, etc.) read *I Wish I Had Someone To Take Up For Me: Help For Those Who Need Hope and Healing*.

4. Make out your own personal "victory list." Unfortunately, human nature makes it easy for us to remember our failures or embarrassing moments. I want to challenge you to write down your *victories* — no matter how small — and regularly review the good things you've done.

chapter 4

BEE A
SELF-
STARTER

 Success or failure can become a habit for all of us. Many people don't succeed because they have a fear of failure.

There's no question that many people never succeed because they're so afraid of failure that they never make an effort to succeed. Fear of failure can be a serious problem. But let me give you some suggestions on how you might overcome your fear of failure so that you will be emotionally released to honestly try for success.

First of all, there are times when you have to simply force yourself to go ahead and try. Just suck it up, grit your teeth, and go ahead. It could be very rewarding to go ahead and make the speech through chattering teeth and shaking knees. (Incidentally, most people won't be able to see your chattering and shaking.)

Second, don't wait around until the situation is perfect before starting a project. Go ahead and start. Quit waiting for the perfect set of circumstances! If you wait until Aunt Matilda moves out, Charlie gets on the day shift, the new governor takes office, the new models are ready, or any other change in the facts outside yourself before you make a commitment to go ahead and do something with your life, then my friend, you will never do more than a fraction of what you're capable of doing.

Overcome fear of failure by starting out with small successes. Start with that first little effort in the right direction. As the Chinese proverb reads, "A journey of a thousand leagues begins with but a single step."*

During my high school years, my brother Richard and his wife had moved to Houston, Texas, in order for him to receive treatments for his heart problem. He invited Martha Ann to come to Houston during the summers, and his wife found Martha a job as a waitress in a nice cafe that was frequented by people who left large tips. We were all amazed when she came home that first fall with new, store-bought dresses, a purse filled with money, and a lifetime of stories about her adventures in the big city.

One night in Houston, Martha waited on Professor and Mrs. Paul Winebrenner of Howard Payne University in Brownwood, Texas. The Winebrenners, who were visiting friends in Houston, thought Martha's southern drawl, conscientious attitude, and beautiful looks shouldn't be relegated to the confines of a small cafe. Here was a girl who should be a teacher.

The Winebrenners wrote to my mama, asking permission to "adopt" Martha long enough to put her through college. Mama didn't know one thing about college, but she *did* know that being a waitress in Houston was the best thing that had ever happened to Martha, so she tried to talk Martha into sticking with the waitress work. But once she realized how much Martha had her heart set on this "college foolishness," she decided to at least let her try.

*From Zig Ziglar's *Steps to the Top* (New York: Pelican, 1985).

Four years later, Martha Ann graduated from Howard Payne University and became a high-school English teacher.

— LIGHTNING STRIKES TWICE —

Almost nothing Martha Ann did really surprised me. I had grown up all my life seeing people bend over backward to help her. She was always loved by her teachers, was the prettiest girl in the class, and made the best grades. Martha Ann could do anything.

I, on the other hand, didn't feel worthy even to walk in Martha's shadow. That's why I was so stunned when Martha came home for a visit after graduating and said to me, "Now, why don't you go to college, Mamie Claire?" *Me! College? She had to be kidding!*

But Martha didn't laugh. She just gave me the name of some people for whom she had baby-sat while working her way through college and told me they would meet me at the bus station if I decided to go. Martha said, "I believe you can do it."

This was one of the first times in my life that anyone said to me, "You can do it." It's difficult, if not impossible, to be a self-starter when you have no concept of doing, being, or having. A kind word of encouragement from Martha was a big step in helping me grow confident enough to be a self-starter.

The year was 1959, and I was twenty years old. I told Mama, "I want to be better, Mama. I think college can make me better. I'm going to give it a try."

And so, with one suitcase, two feedsack dresses, one blouse, a sack of Mama's fried chicken, and twenty-five dollars in cash, I boarded a Greyhound bus and rode 36 hours to Brownwood, Texas.

When the bus finally arrived in Brownwood, it was nightfall. I looked around and thought, *All those lights, and I don't know a soul in this big city.* I was scared to death to be alone in this looming metropolis of 19,453 people. Fortunately, Martha's friends, Dr. and Mrs. Seale Cutbirth, met me at the bus station and helped me get to Howard Payne University.

The next day was registration. There were only three things I didn't know about college back then. I didn't know you had to major. I didn't know you had to minor. And I didn't know you had to pay. So, with the confidence that generally goes with ignorance, I marched off to register for college. I had two dresses, both homemade. One was black with criss-crossed, faded pink flowers, and the other was yellow and black with broad white stripes running through at odd intervals. I wore the pink flowers for registration. A formal occasion called for formal dress.

The registration hall was packed with students. Howard Payne is a Baptist college, and I never dreamed there were that many Baptists in the whole world. (Actually, sometime later, I learned that a few Methodists and Pentecostals had managed to slip in too, but that didn't surprise me, considering there were so many to take care of that day.) I did learn one thing during that first day of registration: If you stand around and look dumb enough long enough, somebody will tell you what to do.

I got into the M line since I was Mamie, but after a half hour of working my way to the front, I was sent to the D line for Darlington. The counselor there was a stick-figured old maid who took one look at my buck teeth, stringy hair, and homemade dress and announced, "You'll probably end up an old maid like me, Mamie Claire. Why don't you go ahead and get a teaching certificate?" I was embarrassed. And every time I got embarrassed,

I broke out in red welts and began to wheeze. Not only was my nose flat and unattractive, which led to the nickname of "Pug" when I was a child, but my small nose also prevented proper air circulation for breathing. As a result, anytime I became the least bit excited, I would hyperventilate and my skin would break out in those large, red welts.

At times when I became embarrassed, I remembered an incident from my childhood Sunday school years. One time the teacher asked me to read out loud the passage of Scripture about the grateful leper who came running back to thank Jesus for helping him. I had gotten so nervous that I began to wheeze and break out in welts as I struggled to read the verse. One little boy in our class looked at me and said, "Wow! That's neat! Not only is she winded and out of breath like the leper, but she also has his splotches. How does she do that?"

That memory and a few others flooded through my mind that day, and I was immediately gasping for breath. All I could do was nod my head in agreement as the old maid signed me up as an education major and scheduled me for the typical freshman courses in that area.

I didn't bother with the financial line that day since I didn't even know what financial meant. But you know what? In college, if you don't pay, eventually they'll send for you. They've got this "thing" about expecting some up-front payback for the future earnings they're going to help you make.

So, I was invited to visit Mr. Garvin, the Vice President of Financial Affairs. I told him who I was and where I had come from.

"What are you doing here all the way from Georgia?" he asked.

"I came to be better," I said.

"How'd you get all this way?"

"By Greyhound bus," I said. (You know he was getting a lot of useful information from me that morning.)

"Tell me, young lady, how do you expect to pay your bill?"

I replied, "I didn't come to pay, I came to work. I heard that you could work your way through college. That's what I aim to do."

"Well, what can you do?" he asked.

I smiled. I was ready for that one. "I can do lots of things. I can crop tobacco, string tobacco, hang tobacco, pick peas, or even sell the *Grit* magazine."

Mr. Garvin flinched. He stared at me. I grew nervous, but thanks to my buck teeth, I just kept smiling.

"Hang and string tobacco?" the man repeated in amazement.

I shook my head. "No, sir," I corrected, "actually, you string it first and then later you — "

"Never mind, never mind," he interrupted. "I'm afraid we don't have anything like that in Brownwood. Look, just tell me, are you going to pay this bill or not?"

"How much is it?" I asked, and as long as I live, I will never forget his answer.

"Exactly $598," he said.

Now I flinched. "Oh, Mr. Garvin," I said, "I don't want to pay everybody's way, just my own."

"That *is* your part," he said. "The cost is $598 every semester for attending classes here."

I almost fainted. *Every* semester! $598! Not only did I not have $598, but I didn't even know anyone else who had that much money. In fact, if you had tried to sell my family by the pound, you wouldn't have gotten $598. I quickly realized I'd made a terrible mistake. I should never have come to college. I lowered my head and walked out of the office.

As I walked back to my dormitory, I remembered Mama's words of advice: "Mamie Claire, you be good at college. That means you say, 'Yes ma'am, no ma'am, thank you, please,' and be polite to your elders." I knew that if I left Howard Payne, out of respect I must let someone know. However, there were some "minor" problems. You see, even self-starters have setbacks. And since I was a novice self-starter, I was concerned.

— HEADED HOME —

I had eaten all my chicken, worn both my dresses, and spent my $25 on books. I needed to get home, but Greyhound didn't take folks collect.

I returned to my dormitory. One of my roommates came in and asked me why I had such slumped shoulders and teary eyes.

"I came all this way to be better, and all I've done is make myself miserable," I said. "I'm going home where a nobody like me belongs."

My roommate smiled. "You're not a nobody, Mamie. This is just your first time away from home. Be a little more patient with yourself. You'll do fine. Come on, cheer up."

"Nothin' to be cheerful about," I said matter-of-factly. "I'm leaving. Who's in charge around here? I need to see him right away."

"In charge? What do you mean?"

"Who do you see when you're thinking of leaving?" I said.

"Oh. Oh, that," said my roommate, thinking I was asking whom I should see to cheer me up and convince me to stay.

"Well, I suppose that would be Dr. Guy Newman."

"Do you need an appointment or can you just go over?"

"I'd call for an appointment. I'm sure he's very busy."

"That many other students pulling out too?" I asked. "Small wonder. The prices are ridiculous."

My roommate stared at me a moment, started to speak, and then gave up. There was no need in telling me I was headed for the office of the college's president. I would only have started wheezing and breaking out.

As the saying goes, "The opera ain't over until the fat lady sings." At Howard Payne University, the withdrawal from admission wasn't over until you met with a counselor. In my naiveté, I had chosen the college president as my withdrawal counselor.

I'll never forget the day I walked into Dr. Newman's office. (He probably never will, either, though for entirely different reasons.) It was September 13, 1959, at two o'clock. I had on high-heeled black pumps that raised my five-feet-nine-inch frame to six feet. I was a size six back then and as skinny as a pole. That day I was wearing my black and yellow dress with the intersecting, broad, white stripes. The stripes were vertical (when you make a dress out of flour sacks, you don't have the option of deciding which way the stripes go) and must have made me look seven feet tall.

Even though I had high heels on, I wasn't wearing hose. I also wasn't wearing any makeup. I was too poor to be able to afford those kinds of luxuries. I used to think hose and makeup were sinful, because I didn't have them. Have you ever noticed how "unsinful" things become once you can afford them? Well, when I didn't have any money, I considered makeup to be sinful. Today, I buy it by the pound.

There I was in Dr. Newman's office, so nervous I began to cry. That made me wheeze and then break out in big, red welts. My hair was frizzled. My feedsack dress was hanging at odd angles. My eyes were gushing tears and getting puffy, but my buck teeth were grinning goofily. I got so nervous my "broke out" was broke out.

Dr. Newman looked apprehensively at me and asked, "Who are you, Miss?"

I wiped a tear, then gasped and wheezed, "Ah'm Mah-mie Clee-air Dol-un-tun from Dix-ay, Joyjuh."

Dr. Newman told me many years later that he took one look at me and thought to himself, *There stands the scrawniest, the homeliest, and the saddest child with the least amount of potential I have ever seen in my entire life...and I have got to encourage her to stay!* Finally, Dr. Newman said, "Mamie Claire, what can I do for you?"

"My Mama needs me back home," I said impulsively, trying to enunciate a little clearer so that my drawl wouldn't need interpreting. "I want to go home."

Dr. Newman folded his hands. "Is your mother ill?"

"No sir, she is very healthy," I assured him.

Dr. Newman thought for a moment and then said, "Well, you've come to Howard Payne for a reason. None of us may know exactly why, but there has got to be a reason. You must understand, Mamie Claire, that while this situation seems very difficult to you right now, life has *many* difficult times. Your life will be fun, exciting, and rewarding, but there *will* be some tough times. You must remember that when the going gets tough, the tough get going — and I don't mean going home. To succeed, Mamie, you must persevere in the face of difficulty. Nothing worth having comes easily."

He paused for a moment to let the message sink in, and then he added, "Now, Mamie, tell me why you decided to come to college in the first place."

"I wanted to be better, that's why," I said.

"And are you better, Mamie?"

I shook my head. "I never got a chance. I barely got signed up before they told me I owed $598. Shucks, my Mama only paid $400 for our whole house, and that took all of us more than six years to pay off. How am I supposed to pay $598 twice a year just to go to school? It's silly to even think about. That's why I've got to get home."

"Have you been attending your classes, Mamie?"

"Yes, sir. I got my books and everything."

"You like college, then?"

"Oh, yes, sir!"

Dr. Newman paused a moment, unclasped his hands, and began

unconsciously to drum the fingers of one hand on the arm of the chair. He seemed lost in thought for a time, then he suddenly turned back to me. "Mamie, I don't want you to leave just yet," he said. "I want you to stay here a few days and continue to attend your classes."

"But why?" I asked.

"Because I believe that you came to Howard Payne for a reason. Just trust me for a few days. I know things won't be easy, but stick it out for a while."

You see, our job is not to judge. I have a sign in my kitchen that reads, LOVE MORE AND JUDGE LESS. We could change the world if everyone believed and lived that philosophy. As educators, parents, and employers, we have the responsibility and opportunity of encouraging others.

That day in 1959, Dr. Newman could easily have dismissed me as an insignificant interruption in his overcrowded schedule. There was no way for him to have predicted that I would graduate from college and make something of my life. Fortunately for me, Dr. Newman understood that it takes only one person to believe in someone for him or her to succeed. He recognized that many people have gone further than they thought they could because someone else thought they could. I thank God for Dr. Newman and for his being that someone else at that critical point in my life.

I left and went back to the dorm. The next day, Dr. and Mrs. Newman came to visit me at my room. Mrs. Newman sat down next to me, took my hand, and said, "Mamie, I understand that you have financial problems."

I still didn't know what financial meant, but I nodded and said,

"Yes, ma'am." I had every other kind of problem, so I figured I must have financial problems too.

"My wife and I would like you to live at our home this year, Mamie," Dr. Newman said. "You would be our guest. You could go to school and line up some part-time jobs. Once you are on your feet, you could pay your bills and move back to the dorm and be with your new friends."

Now, let me ask you: If you were 1,250 miles from home, had worn both your dresses, had eaten all your fried chicken, and had spent your life savings of $25, what would you have done if the college president and his wife had invited you to live with them? You would have jumped at the chance, right? Of course. Any sane person would have. Guess what I did, though? I said, "I'll think about it and let you know."

Even though I was learning to be a self-starter, at this point I had never made a decision by myself in my whole life. I always asked Mama before I did anything. Mama's advice wasn't always the perfect guidance, but she was blessed with wisdom far beyond her education. There was always comfort in her counsel. So, I called home.

HEARTITUDE:

See others as they can be

— not as they are.

♡

There were only nine phones in Dixie, Georgia, and it took me three days to clear the party lines and get Mama to a phone. She heard my story, then said, "You can go live there, Mamie, but you be sure to help that woman in any way you can. You can accept their help, but you can work too." I promised I would.

— WHEN YOU DON'T KNOW HOW TO DO SOMETHING, START —

I lived that year with the Newmans. Their water came from a tap, their heat was from a gas furnace, and the only gardening Mrs. Newman did was to keep American Beauty roses around the trellis of their porch. So the chores Mama told me to do were out of the question. I did find some work elsewhere, however.

Knowing that I was a hard worker, Dr. Newman went into Brownwood one day to visit a successful Christian businessman named Herman Bennett. Mr. Bennett was a burly man who owned a contracting company as well as several smaller enterprises. "Herman, there's a little gal who is going to have to quit college and go home to Georgia if she can't find work before Christmas," Dr. Newman told his friend. "What you desperately need around your office is a secretary. Would you hire this girl as your secretary for awhile?"

Mr. Bennett, always a friend of the University and of Dr. Newman personally, said he would give me a try.

The interesting thing about this arrangement was that there were only two people in Brownwood, Texas, who didn't know what a secretary was supposed to do. Mr. Bennett was one, and I was the other. I had worked as a typist for a while in Georgia, but I had never been trained as a receptionist, office manager, phone operator, or stenographer. As for Mr. Bennett, he had done most of his business on the phone, in person, or via his attorney or accountant. So I showed up for work not knowing what to do, and I was met by a boss who had no idea of what I could or should do.

Fortunately, I had been raised to "find something to do" whenever I had any spare time — the beginnings of my life as a self-starter. So I grabbed a broom and swept the office, and that made Mr. Bennett smile. Then I fixed a pot of coffee, and he seemed pleased about that too. Next, I found a cloth and I dusted everything. Then I emptied the wastebaskets.

After all that, Mr. Bennett left the office for a couple of hours to conduct some work-site inspections. When he got back, I had taken six phone messages for him, washed his office windows, and cleaned his coffee cup.

"Mamie, you and I are going to get along fine," Mr. Bennett announced. "I live by one rule: *If you don't know how to do something, start* (the self-starter's credo). You sure seem to know all about that. I'm really impressed with your drive and ambition. You are a lucky young lady.

"I am going to teach you how to be a businesswoman. You may have come to Howard Payne with the idea of being a teacher, but I guarantee you, you'll wind up an executive."

Mr. Bennett stayed true to his word. He taught me all he could about cash flow management, advertising, public relations, contract negotiations, real estate purchases, business controls, and personnel supervision. His wife, Chloe, was equally interested in my welfare. She added to my knowledge of how to cook, care for a large house, sew, and use my creativity to develop homemaking skills.

During my year of living with Dr. and Mrs. Guy Newman, I was sent to a charm school, where I learned how to use makeup, walk in a dignified way, and select clothes that were more flattering to my figure. I was even hired as a part-time model for a local clothing store because I was so tall and thin. During my junior and senior years, thanks to a barter agreement I worked out with the clothing store and to doing well at baby-sitting, I was voted the best-dressed girl on campus. (Actually, the certificate read, "Most Pleasing to Behold" because Howard Payne is a Baptist school, and we didn't want to seem too worldly.)

You may be thinking, "Well, I could be a self-starter too, if people were doing as much for me as they did for Mamie." And if you're thinking that way, you're at least partially correct. Many people were very good to me. But no matter how good people are to you, if you won't take advantage of your opportunities, life will pass right by you. Neighbors can share all the food with you that you might possibly eat, but you must take action on the gift by accepting and eating.

I could have accepted the help of others with a poor attitude and made little or nothing of my opportunities. However, because of some "deep-down" self-starter characteristics, I seized the opportunity. I believe you have similar opportunities. Regardless of your situation, someone wants to help you. It may be your parents, brother or sister, co-workers, boss, principal, manager, or supervisor, but *someone* is there to help. Why not be a self-starter and *start* by accepting the help and saying "thank you" by taking action.

If you work hard, you'll justify the kindnesses others have shown you. I worked as hard in the next few months and years as I have ever worked in my life; hard work is another self-starter characteristic.

I moved back into the dorm when I was a sophomore. I worked

for Mr. Bennett in the afternoons, went to college in the mornings, took in laundry at night for extra money, held a position as a dorm director, and baby-sat on weekends. I did my homework late at night and during the hours I was baby-sitting. My days often began at 4:00 a.m. and weren't over until midnight.

The results were worth every bit of the effort. I had come to college "to be better." Thanks to my professors, the Newmans, the Bennetts, the Cutbirths, and other people I had come in contact with in Brownwood, Texas, I truly was becoming a better person. People showed affection to me, and I returned affection. People showed trust in me, and I worked hard to merit trust. People gave me opportunities, and I capitalized upon them. Dr. Newman had said that there had to have been a reason for me to come to Brownwood. After several years, I learned he was right.

HEARTITUDE:

If you don't know

how to do something,

START.

— MAKING A FUTURE —

After I graduated with a teaching degree in business education in the summer of 1963, Mr. Bennett asked me to join his company on a full-time basis.

"I surely am grateful for that offer, Mr. Bennett, but I guess I need to try some new experiences and look for new challenges," I answered him.

"Good," he said. "Here's your first one." With that, he handed me a ring of keys.

"What's this?" I asked.

"I just bought a 13-story hotel down the street," he explained. "And I've appointed you general manager of the place."

"Manager? Hotel?" I stammered. "But I don't know anything about managing a hotel, Mr. Bennett."

He grinned at me, then chided me with, "If you don't know how to do something, start. You'll learn. I know you. But learn quickly. That's only one of your new responsibilities. You're also going to supervise the construction of some new apartment buildings I plan to erect this autumn."

And that was that.

I worked part-time for Mr. Bennett during the four years I was in college, and then for six more years on a full-time basis. I eventually became Vice President of Bennett Construction Company and gained invaluable business experience. As I look back, this was one of the most rewarding times of my entire life.

I learned a lot of useful skills from the Newmans and Bennetts — everything from how to behave like a lady to how to manage people. But the most important thing I learned from them was to show *all* others compassion, love, and patience. Had these dear people judged Mamie Claire Darlington on her appearance in 1959, I never would have had a chance to reach my potential as a human being. They didn't judge, however. They simply showed compassion, love, and patience.

I can truthfully say that these people had more confidence in my potential than I did myself. They were gracious enough not to label me. To them, I was never "Pug," "Monkey," "Martha's sister, what's-her-name," "one of those poor Darlington kids," "hick," or "old maid." I was a human being worthy of all the dignity that any soul should be afforded.

The Reverend Jesse Jackson tells his audiences, "It is your attitude, not your aptitude, that determines your altitude in life." He's right. You can soar high in life, even if you don't have an IQ of 180. Remember: the secret is to develop a self-starter's attitude.

Winners like the Newmans, Bennetts, Joneses, and many others helped me develop a winner's attitude. Who are you helping to overcome obstacles in life? Who are you believing in when they can't believe in themselves? To whom are you showing compassion, love, and patience? Who are you helping to develop the winner's attitude and become a self-starter? Be a self-starter by starting now to help others.

— I CAN...AND *HERE'S HOW* YOU CAN TOO! —

1. "Bee a Self-Starter." Belief in others and belief in self, planning, politeness, ambition, courage to accept and act, hard work, and faith are all self-starter characteristics. And most importantly, when you don't know how to do something, *start*. Overcome the paralysis of analysis holding others back. Take action! Do it now!

2. Please remember: Nothing worth having comes easily. Persevere in the face of difficulty.

3. Love more and judge less. We can change the world if we believe and live this philosophy. Begin by seeing others as they can be, not as they are.

4. Show *all* people compassion, love, and patience. Do unto others as you would like them to do unto you.

5. Practice Random Acts of Kindness: Smile. Speak to strangers. Send appreciation notes and even flowers. Pick up the tab for a less fortunate stranger at a restaurant. These Random Acts of Kindness don't have to cost a lot of money. Just help others to know that they are special and important!

chapter 5

BEE A
RESPONDER

So many times in our lives, things happen to us that we have no control over. What we're held responsible for is how we react or respond to the situation.

There's a difference between responding and reacting. Several years ago, I developed a rash on the left side of my face. I couldn't tell if I had an allergy, an infection, or something else. So, my secretary made an appointment for me to see a dermatologist in the city I was headed to for a speaking engagement.

The dermatologist examined my face and asked, "How old are you?" Don't you think it was tacky for a doctor who had just met me to ask such a personal question?

"Forty-something," I replied.

"That's it!" he said. "It's your age!"

I asked him how it could be my age — the right side of my face was the same age, and it wasn't broken out! Then he told me my problem was just a temporary hormonal imbalance. He said the rash was quite common in women my age. For good measure, however, he said he wanted to take some cultures, run some tests, and have me come back for the next three days for observation.

"That's not possible," I explained. "I'm booked solidly for the rest of the week. Please just give me a prescription so that I can get my face cleared up."

After a little arguing, and against his better judgment, the physician finally yielded to my pressure and went ahead and wrote a prescription for me. I started taking the medication every four hours, fully expecting my body to respond to the treatment right away.

The next morning, I thought I would look in the mirror and see both sides of my face looking normal. Instead, it turned out that I was allergic to the drug I was taking and both sides of my face were now puffy, painful, and covered with the rash. My body had not responded to the medication, it had reacted. To react is negative. I then went back to the doctor, apologized for trying to tell him how to do his job, and let him run his tests. He gave me a different prescription, and by the weekend I was much better. I responded to the proper treatment; however, responding took two weeks. To respond is positive. It's always easier and quicker to react than to respond, but the wise option is to respond.

We cannot change what happens to us in life, but we can choose whether we respond positively to each situation or react negatively. We can decide what there is to learn and how we can pass the experience on and help others. So many times when something happens, we think we're the only people in the world with that problem. We don't choose the circumstances, we choose our response — or reaction. So, don't react with self-pity or bitterness or defeatism when life deals you a low blow. Instead, respond to it by thinking positively, acting responsibly, and staying optimistic.

Two years after I graduated from college, I learned how difficult it could be to respond instead of react. I don't think anyone wanted marriage and children more than I did at that time. I was lonely, and at twenty-six years old I felt I was well on the way to becoming an old maid.

I met Don McCullough when I was twenty-four. The first time I ever saw him, I knew he was what I wanted in a man. He was a Southern Baptist Christian, well-educated, and a perfect gentleman. The problem was, I never made a point of telling Don I considered him my ideal man. So, Don and I dated on and off for eight and a half years, but nothing serious developed. Actually, we didn't date often. Don was a busy college professor, and he was working toward his doctorate. He was also very involved in church work and youth ministry. Listening to the advice of friends, I decided that he would never ask me to marry him because he was so involved in college and other activities.

During this time, I was also occasionally dating other young men. In 1965, I met a man I liked a lot. In my day, we called him a "city slicker," and maybe that's what attracted Mamie Darlington to him. A man *that* well-dressed, well-groomed, and "polished" had never taken an interest in me before.

I wanted a home and children so badly that when he asked me to marry him, I said yes. I had dated him on and off for three years. We were married in the fall of 1968 and stayed right in Brownwood, since he was a traveling salesman and could live anywhere in his territory. At the same time, I could continue working for Mr. Bennett.

Though my new husband had "hinted" that he was not as interested as I was in a home and children, I was optimistic that I could change his mind. After four months of marriage, however, my niece Amy, who was about four years old, came to visit us, and I learned just how much he detested children. You cannot imagine how disappointed I was. The one dream I had had since youth seemed to be slipping away. If you have ever had that terrible "sinking feeling" in your stomach as you face impending disaster, you'll know how I felt at the moment I learned his true feelings about children.

Another problem soon became apparent. My husband wanted me to work because I was making good money, but he resented the long hours and the tenants' continual calls at any hour that a faucet happened to leak. I knew he wasn't entirely satisfied with our marriage, but I clung to the hope that we could work out our problems.

On May 5, 1969, my sister Martha Ann called my office. Her son, Claude, who was only three months old, had been stricken with meningitis. I will never forget her grief-stricken words: "Mamie Claire, Claude may not live through the night. Can you come to Houston and help me?" My love and respect for Martha had always outweighed any jealousy I felt toward her, so I hurried home to pack my clothes.

When I arrived at our apartment, another shock was waiting for me. A note was pinned crudely next to the numbers on the door. It read: "I'm sorry, I cannot accept the responsibilities of marriage. I have moved out."

Unless you have had the wind knocked out of you by a kick in the stomach, you cannot imagine how I felt at that moment. All I had experienced when I was abused as a child — the nausea, the fear, the "dirty" feelings — swept over me like an ice cold winter wind. The inferior feelings I had felt when I started college, the mocking of grade-school children, the embarrassment of hand-me-down clothes — everything negative that I had ever experienced flashed through my mind in one sickening instant.

My sister and her son needed me, however, and I couldn't dwell on my problems. I didn't know where my husband had gone, but I knew I had to go to Martha Ann, so I drove more than three hundred miles, crying every inch of the trip. Little Claude did live, though severely brain-damaged. When I arrived in Houston and saw the look in my sister's eyes, I knew I had made the right choice in going to be with her.

Shortly after my return to Brownwood, my husband came back, saying he was sorry. "I think our problem is both of us working. If you'll just quit your job and travel with me, we can spend more time together and be happy," he said. I had worked with Mr. Bennett for nearly ten years, but I knew that my marriage must come first. So, I resigned my position at my husband's request.

Our first trip together was a two-week swing into the Texas Valley. I relaxed for the first time in many years and enjoyed the pool and the peace and quiet of "slow-moving" days with no deadlines to meet, while my husband made sales calls. I can truthfully say that I enjoyed the two weeks of rest and relaxation.

One night just a few days after we returned to Brownwood, we were finishing dinner when my husband pushed his plate away and looked over at me. "I'm sorry," he said. "We're going to have to get the divorce. I'm just not happy."

As I lay in bed that night, I realized that you could not make people love you. I had married for the wrong reasons. I married for what I wanted the relationship to be, not what it really was. There are no words to express the heartache I felt at being a "failure."

— LIFE GOES ON —

I spent the rest of the summer and fall in my apartment. I wouldn't talk to anyone. I felt as if I had let down those people in Brownwood who had loved and taught me. Certainly, I was an embarrassment to my family. Not one of our close relatives had ever been divorced. I was going through a time of grief that was natural and probably inevitable to some extent, but I was also reacting rather than responding to my situation.

That fall, the Chamber of Commerce and companies in the community offered me jobs in Brownwood, but I rejected their offers. The fourth time, however, the Chamber called with an assignment I couldn't resist. "We're building a state school for girls here in Brownwood," said Dr. Bill Doggett, the director of the project, "and we want you because of your experience to oversee the construction of the buildings and their decoration." This sounded like a job that would be challenging and rewarding, so I accepted.

I worked like crazy in an attempt to keep my mind off my "failure." I did everything from hiring the new staff to selecting the colors for the interior decorating. That was fine during the days, but at nights I still had to go home to an empty apartment and, thus, had to face an empty life.

The holiday season made me feel even more alone. Eventually, I gave up. "I have so many aunts and cousins and nieces and nephews and sisters at home," I explained to Dr. Doggett.

"I don't have any family here. I'm going to Georgia to be with my mother."

I went back to Dixie right before Christmas. I thought I would sit on Mama's front porch and rock until I died. I refused to see my old friends. I stopped eating. I wouldn't read or watch television or go for a ride or cook meals or talk. All I wanted to do was fall off the face of the earth.

Finally, after a few months, my anger sent me into a frenzy of activity. I went out one day and bought a car trunk load of decorating supplies and hired a carpenter to help me. Together, we remodeled Mama's house, and then I repainted and wallpapered. I was obsessed with the idea of changing her home so it wouldn't remind me of a scene from my past.

(In December of 1968, barely two months after our marriage, I had brought my new husband home to meet my family. It was Christmas, and I was a newlywed. Things should have been exciting and joyous. Instead, my husband was bored by our kitchen table conversations and reminiscences and irritated that Christmas to us revolved around the local Baptist church. He called my relatives "dumb hillbillies" and made fun of the way they talked and acted. He insisted that we return to Texas only a few days after we had arrived.)

Mama was delighted to have her home all redecorated before the holiday season rolled around, but it upset her to see me work with such a vengeance at changing everything. I was reacting like a disturbed and unstable woman. My moods were unpredictable. At first, I had gone for weeks saying and doing nothing; then, suddenly, I had started working 20 hours a day at redecorating the entire house. My life had no balance, no sense of continuity. Yet my family loved me through my moods and heartaches and helped in every way they could to encourage me.

My decision to marry had been a mistake, and I didn't want to be reminded of my error. I've made other mistakes since then; I'll certainly make even more before the good Lord calls me home. But one thing I've learned through all this is: *Making a mistake is no excuse for living as a mistake.*

— OTHERS HAVE RESPONDED —

I have counseled people of all ages from all walks of life who have made mistakes — serious ones — that have convinced them that their only solution was to die. I know that feeling. I've been there. I've talked with youngsters who have had to tell their parents about things that are devastating: illegitimate pregnancy, a dependency on drugs, involvement in a car theft ring, a homosexual encounter, a fraternity initiation that led to a prison sentence, a desertion of country to avoid the draft. In each case, the humiliation seemed unbearable and the sense of personal failure overwhelming.

HEARTITUDE:

Making a mistake is no excuse for living as a mistake.

♡

On a different level, the same sorts of serious mistakes are being made by supposedly mature adults. People have told me their stories and asked, "But how could it have happened to me?" I've known of a public official who was a child abuser, a minister who tried to seduce the ladies of his congregation, a corporate president who embezzled company funds, an ambulance driver who stole money from injured people's wallets, and an attorney who tricked elderly clients into deeding him land in their wills. When caught in these immoral or illegal activities, each person wished he or she could just die. In fact, some chose suicide rather than having to face their friends and relatives again.

Perhaps you may be going through a similar situation. Maybe you know someone else who is. We all have feet of clay. Failure and rejection are things we find hard to deal with. Lee Iacocca said that after he was fired as president of the Ford Motor Company, he couldn't look his children in the face for days. Yet he rallied his courage and became Chairman of Chrysler Corporation, making an even greater name for himself as a leader.

We must learn to pull ourselves back together after we've made a mistake and go ahead with new self-confidence and strength. We must learn to respond instead of react.

— A NEW EDUCATION —

In my case, one of the things that kept me from living as a mistake was getting back to work and realizing that I still had something to offer people. The town of Dixie, Georgia, didn't have a local school, so about this time, some of the parents got together and decided to provide a private school for their children. They asked me if I would be one of their teachers.

That summer I took a six-week course in Georgia history so I could get my state teaching certificate. I also helped the parents restore the old school building, which I had attended as a child and which had been closed in the late 1950s during a consolidation of the district. One day we were cleaning the basement and came across the old school trophies stored in a box. Would our basketball trophy be there? I wondered. After a couple minutes of looking, I found the small trophy that was so large in my memory, with the names Elizabeth Jones, Mamie Claire Darlington, and Therlisel Webb engraved on it. Months later, when Elizabeth Jones, the music and English teacher who had been "the rich girl up on the hard road," Therlisel Webb, the school secretary whose father owned "one of the two stores in Dixie," and Mamie Claire Darlington, the business teacher who used to be "one of those Darlington kids," walked into the renovated building together, I felt equal to them for the first time.

As I walked into my class, I was flooded with memories of all the respect and love I had for the teachers who trained me in this same building. Now, I was one of those very special women I had grown up admiring so dearly, a school teacher in Dixie, Georgia.

The highschool boys who sat in that room were almost men. Some of them were rough and tough from years of farming and fending for themselves. But they looked at me with eager anticipation. I was their teacher. They knew nothing about my background. That day, I started seeing myself as a very special lady, at least before the kids. And for the time, that was enough to bring me out of my shell. I began to be happy that God had not answered my "death-wish" prayer. God's plans and His timing are *always* right. Over the years, I have learned that He never makes a mistake.

— MAMA KNOWS BEST —

As the weeks passed and my disposition improved, Mama began to formulate a plan that, if it worked, would make me the happiest woman in Georgia.

Mama knew that I had always been in love with Don McCullough. Although she had met Don only briefly, she liked him and wanted him as a son-in-law. Everything I had ever said about Don was music to her ears: Don's parents were former missionaries, Don was a college professor and a church leader, Don was always a gentleman.

One day when I came home from school, Mama was waiting with her camera. She told me to sit down on the couch and to smile. "What's going on here, Mama?" I asked.

"We're going to see if your old beau is still carrying a torch for you," said Mama as she snapped the shutter on the camera. "Keep smiling. I want to get some different angles."

"Old beau? Carrying a torch? Whatever are you talking about, Mama?"

"Don McCullough," she said, clicking off another picture. "I'm willing to bet that he's still interested in you. I want you to write him a letter and tell him where you are now. And send one of these pictures. I'm having you sit on the couch so that I can get the clock on the wall in the background. Don gave you that clock. If he sees that you still have it, he'll figure you still remember him."

I stood up and waved off the camera idea. "This is ridiculous," I protested. "There's no way in the world that I'm going to write Don McCullough. First of all, he was never all that interested in me to begin with. Secondly, there's no way that the son of a Baptist preacher is going to want anything to do with a divorced woman."

Mama put her hands on my shoulders and gently pushed me back down on the couch. "I thought you would say something like that. But you and me got this thing figured differently, Mamie

Claire. Let me tell you how I see this situation.

"Don was raised in South America as a missionary kid. He didn't get the same chances to go on dates and to school shindigs when he was a teenager the way you and other kids here in America did. I believe he's shy. He's never really had a good chance to learn about dating."

I rolled my eyes. "Oh, Mama, be serious," I said. "The man is a college professor in psychology. He was licensed as a pilot at an early age. He speaks Spanish better than we speak English. We're not talking about some young, wet-behind-the-ears kid, here. Don McCullough has been around."

"I don't care if he's been to Timbuktu and back, I still say he's probably shy and that he's still in love with you," insisted Mama. "I may not have all that fancy book learnin' that you've got, but that don't mean I haven't learned a thing or two about men in my time. Now, I want you to write that man a letter and send him these pictures."

I didn't know whether to laugh or cry, whether to be grateful to Mama over her concern or mad at her for butting in where she didn't belong. I decided to try to reason with her. "Mama, I appreciate what you're trying to do," I said slowly, "but no matter how much picture-taking and letter-writing we do, we're not going to be able to change the fact that I'm a divorced woman. I made my mistake, now I've got to live with the consequences."

Mama moved over to where I was seated. She put her face right up close to mine. "You hear me out, Mamie Claire. There has never been a finer girl than you are, child. I raised you good, and you grew up good, and you *are* good. I know that, your brothers and sisters know that, and if Don McCullough has half a lick of sense about him, then he knows that too. If you two young folks are in love, you ought to be together."

"But, Mama, what about my — "

"Your divorce?" interrupted Mama. "Well, what about it? The Good Book says there ain't no forgiveness for divorce unless the one you're married to commits adultery. In that case, divorce is sad but justified. That scoundrel you was married to was chasin' everything in a skirt before, during, and after you were married. He wrote you a note saying he wouldn't stay faithful to you. That's what you've got to explain to Don McCullough when you write to him."

My stomach began to knot. I could feel a tension headache coming on. "Mama...I...I just...don't know," I stammered, feeling confused and quite overwhelmed. "It could all end up so embarrassing. I could look like a fool."

"That's true, that's true," said Mama, reaching over to pat my hand. "But I'd risk being a fool every day of my life if I thought there was a chance in a million I could get back together with your daddy. I don't even have a chance. But you do, Mamie Claire. And the only way you are going to wind up being a fool is if you don't take your one chance. Try it, girl. Try it. A good man is worth risking your pride for."

I looked up and stared at Mama. Her eyes were warm and sincere. She desperately wanted to see me find happiness. At that instant I decided to throw caution to the wind. I smiled and said, "Pick up that camera, Mama. Get some shots of my good side. Let's show that Don McCullough what he's missing."

I Can. You Can Too!

I wrote the letter on November 1, but I still couldn't bring myself to send it to Don, so I compromised and mailed it to his parents. That seemed less "pushy" to me. Besides, I knew they would show the letter to Don. If he was interested, I would soon know. But Don didn't call. His parents sent me a very kind and cordial response, but no word came from Don. I waited all month, but he didn't write to me. I tried to put up a good front, but Mama knew I was heartbroken. I worked overtime at the school in an effort to lose myself in my work and, thus, suppress my feeling of disappointment over Don's callousness. *At least he could have dropped me a card,* I told myself.

My aggravation grew as the weeks passed. Finally, in mid-January, Don called and asked if he could visit me in February. I pretended to be somewhat indifferent, but my heart was pounding like mad!

In mid-February, at the end of a normal school day, I looked up from my desk and made eye contact with Don McCullough. "Hello, Mamie," he said as he held out a single red rose. "I've been waiting for you."

I was so stunned that, for the moment, I couldn't speak. Finally, I found my voice. "*You've* been waiting for *me?*" I retorted. "I wrote to your parents more than three months ago. I've been waiting for you!"

Don's face turned red. He glanced around and then back to me. "Well, actually," he said, "when your letter arrived, I was out of town. Then, as soon as I got back, I found your letter and I phoned you, packed up, and left as soon as possible. Besides, I guess I'm just old-fashioned, but I wanted to propose face to face."

"Well, old-fashioned or not, I still say you could have —"

I stopped in mid-sentence and stood there with my mouth open. "Did you say propose?" I finally whispered.

Don nodded. "If you'll have me. I asked your mother. She's given us her blessing."

On February 14, 1971, I said yes to the man of my dreams, Don McCullough.

— HAPPY DAYS —

On June 4 of that year (Don's parents' anniversary), we were married in the Dixie Baptist Church. My sisters were my bridesmaids, and my entire class of students witnessed the ceremony from the front three pews. The rich folks up on the hard road were there too. I was 32 years old, and Don was 36. Elizabeth sang, and "Mr. Carl Winter" gave me away.

My previous marriage had been a mistake, but thanks to Mama and Don McCullough, I no longer had to live as a mistake. The day I married Don McCullough was without a doubt the happiest day of my life.

Don was forever indebted to my mother for what she had done to get us back together. To that end, we decided to live and work in Georgia so that we could take care of her and be with her in her declining years. This was no small sacrifice on Don's part. It not only meant that he had to resign his position as a college professor in Texas, but also that he had to stop working on the completion of his doctoral dissertation (the only thing remaining for the Ph.D. he so desired). Additionally, he was now nearly 1,200 miles away from his own parents.

I worked hard to make Don not regret his choice. I took a job as the vocational office training teacher at Central High School at $5,500 per year and worked in the school system from 1971 until 1979. I learned to cook Don's favorite foods, and I kept house too. I gave birth to our first child, Patti, in March, 1973; our second child, Brian, in April, 1975; and our third child, Jennifer, in September, 1976. I worked each time until the day before the child was born, and I was back on the job within a few weeks afterward.

Don worked hard too. He became a staff psychologist for three counties in Georgia. He directed the psychological tests for all families that asked for federal assistance, and he served as an advisor for crisis situations in the school systems. Many, many times we were awakened in the middle of the night by a knock on our door by some runaway youngster, battered wife, unemployed husband, deserted spouse, or alcoholic grandparent. Don gave them a listening ear, a word of prayer, and some sincere advice. We turned no one away.

Don and I developed a deep love for our students. We worked out our own approaches to teaching and testing and encouraging and disciplining the students we worked with. Other counselors used Don's techniques for dealing with troubled youngsters, and other teachers used my procedures for motivating students to want to learn.

I had no way of knowing back then that these early practices of ours would one day lead us to write, market, and teach a whole new approach to learning, *The I CAN Way of Life*. Truly, I had no idea that just ahead of me lay the greatest triumphs of my life.

— I CAN...AND *HERE'S HOW* YOU CAN TOO! —

1. "Bee a Responder." You can learn to respond positively rather than react negatively. Don't react with self-pity, bitterness, or defeatism. Instead, respond by thinking positively, acting positively, and staying optimistic.

2. Making a mistake is no excuse for living as a mistake. Work hard, persevere, stay busy, keep your options open, and you can overcome mistakes.

3. There is a major difference between making a mistake and being a failure. When I finally understood the difference, it changed my life.

4. Believe in yourself, persevere, and succeed!

chapter 6

BEE A GOAL- SETTER

If you're playing a game of basketball, you have baskets (the goals of the game) on each end. You have a scorekeeper and a timekeeper. I believe that when you're playing the game of life, you also have to have goals or you cannot tell whether you're winning or losing.

Goals should be planned for all aspects of life: physical, mental, spiritual, financial, career, social, and family. One of the mandatory assignments for my high-school students was, they had to dream the big dream. "Before the end of the year, you have to tell me what your big dream is," I'd say. "You can either write it, tell me privately, or tell the entire class if you want to." Toward the end of one semester in 1974, Dalerie, a tall, thin, black girl who was shy but very sweet, came up to me after class. She was quivering as she said, "Mrs. McCullough, I just cannot tell you my big dream. I'll just have to fail the class."

"But, Dalerie," I protested, "I know you have a dream. Just share it with me."

She stepped back a little and said, "I'll talk to you later." Then she was gone.

A few days later, Dalerie came up to me again. "Mrs. McCullough, you're not going to believe my big dream."

"Oh, yes I am, Dalerie. Please tell me."

Big tears were flowing down her cheeks as she said, "Mrs. McCullough, I would like to be a doctor."

"Dalerie, I think that's just wonderful!"

"Oh, but Mrs. McCullough, you have to understand. No one in my family has ever graduated from high school. And I don't really live with my family. I live with an aunt. I don't believe I can be a doctor, but that's my big dream."

Unfortunately, so many young people have so labeled themselves that they don't feel they can achieve their goals. Dalerie was halfway to becoming what she wanted to be before she was able to verbalize her goal in life.

Dalerie graduated from college. I don't know where she is now, but I do know she finished with her associate bachelor's degree. She set her goal and was able to reach way beyond her family's previous educational accomplishments.

Do you know what you're living for? Do you know what your goals are? Do you know the score? Are you winning or losing the game?

Do you know what you want on your tombstone? Don McCullough used to laugh and say he was going to put, "She did it and got it over with" on mine.

After I had Patti, our first baby, I seriously considered the idea of staying home. Life was wonderful, and I had everything I ever wanted. I had a wonderful husband, a new house, and a baby. I found out something about myself, however. I don't like to admit it, but I'm going to go ahead and confess to you: I do *not* like housework! I love my children and my home. I also love to cook. But there are just a few things about homemaking that I don't like — mopping and sweeping, making beds, washing clothes, dusting and waxing furniture, and ironing. I have never been motivated by cleaning a commode in my life (no matter how pretty the color).

I have my own theories about housekeeping. I've always believed that dust was meant to be a protective coating for furniture. I used to keep a few get-well cards on my television so that if people dropped by unexpectedly and saw that the house was a mess, they would assume that was just because I had been ill lately.

When Patti was two months old, I confessed to Don that I didn't like doing housework. Don was always very practical. He replied, "Well, Mamie, we cannot afford to hire someone to do the house-work for you on only one salary. You have a choice: stay home and clean, or work outside the home."

I thought about that choice all morning. I knew that Don hadn't mentioned our responsibility to help support Mama, which I also had to consider.

That afternoon I called the superintendent of schools and told him I was ready to go back to teaching at the high school. There was a slight pause, and then he informed me as graciously as possible that my old job was no longer open. I reminded him that I had tenure. He reminded me that I had resigned. I looked around my kitchen and saw the stack of dirty dishes and the unwaxed linoleum. I swallowed hard and then, in my sweetest and most persuasive voice, I asked the superintendent if he had any other openings.

"Just one," he said. "I need a teacher for the eighth grade."

"Junior high?" I gasped. "Eighth grade? Are students potty trained at that age? Is that all you have?"

"It's that or nothing."

One more glance at the stacked dishes convinced me to say, "I'll take it."

"Fine. Report in August...and good luck."

I replaced the receiver and thought to myself, *One down and one to go.* Now, who else could I get to hire me? Don was right when he figured that a Georgia teaching salary wouldn't be enough to enable me to hire a baby-sitter for Patti and a cleaning woman for the house, as well as cover the expenses of clothes, gasoline, and other job-related expenses.

My experience in the business community as Vice President of Herman Bennett's construction company had taught me a great deal about hiring, firing, buying, selling, and the importance of making a profit. I learned that some of the best paid individuals in our society are in the business of direct sales. Consequently, I determined that my "second" job needed to be in the world of selling.

I had also learned several important things about choosing a business or company with which to work. Number one, there must be an unquestionable belief in the products or services being offered. Number two, the products or services must meet an ongoing need. Number three, the ethics of the people involved in the organization must be above reproach. And number four, you must enjoy the activities that yield results in the chosen business.

As I began to evaluate products and services in my life, I found a product I truly believed in and was using myself; the product met an ongoing need; and, the ethics of the people involved were above reproach. Since the only way to be successful with this particular company was by helping others to be more successful, I knew I had found the right product for me. I love people! Talking to them about a product I believed in would be quite natural for me. So I approached the person I knew who worked with this company and boldly asked if they needed an excited, motivated person. To my great delight, the dear lady I approached had been wanting to recruit me for her business for some time! I had my second income!

Once I secured those two jobs and hired someone to baby-sit and clean house, I had a new lease on life. Everything was fun for me once again. I enjoyed being with my students each day, and I worked enough at selling in the evening to pay for the outside help I had hired. My life was going extremely well.

— GAINING MOMENTUM —

In the fall of 1973, my regional manager began talking about a national convention to be held in Atlanta in January of 1974. Having never been to one of the national conventions, I asked what the program would be like and who would be speaking.

"Zig Ziglar," she replied.

I screwed up my face and asked, "Zig-Zagger? What do you do with it, sew clothes or wash dishes?"

"No, no, Zig isn't a product," she explained. "Zig Ziglar is a *person*. He built his reputation as a salesman and then went on to write best-selling books about sales procedures and personal growth. Today, he's one of the most sought-after motivational teachers in America."

Well, as it turned out, Zig was utterly incredible. There's an old expression that says, "When the student is ready, the teacher will appear." I was the ready student that January 31, 1974, and Zig Ziglar was the teacher who appeared.

More than four thousand women were gathered in the Hilton Hotel ballroom that day. I, somehow, had been given a seat on the very front row. I was right in the middle of all the music, chanting, hand-clapping, laughing, and cheering. The enthusiasm was unbelievable. I had never seen such unleashed exuberance in all my life.

Then the house lights went down and the spotlight hit the stage, and Zig Ziglar came bounding forward. He was greeted by applause and whistling. In fact, he received a standing ovation even before he spoke.

HEARTITUDE:

When the student is ready, the teacher will appear.

♡

For the next three hours, Zig gave a rapid-fire address that carried one central message: You can go where you want to go, you can do what you want to do, and you can be what you want to be — with the proper input! He may have been speaking to four thousand women, but it seemed as though his message was aimed at me alone!

On the flight home from Atlanta (I was so inspired, I don't think I really needed the airplane), I thought to myself, I'd love to be one of those women on the stage who was recognized for achievement at the convention. I even wanted to have a suede suit, as they had. I knew it would probably take me three years to pay for such a suit from my teacher's salary, so the only option was to earn it through direct sales.

When I got home I asked Don, "Do you think I could be one of those award winners?"

"What do you think?" Don asked me. You know psychologists: They always answer a question with a question.

I said, "Well, they have two legs and I have two legs. They have two arms and I have two. I have one head and they do too. And if they've got something else I haven't got, I'm sure I can get me one or have mine fixed."

I called my manager and asked her what I had to do to be a sales manager, like the women on the platform. She gave me all the necessary details.

I wrote all the information down as she talked. Then I asked a crucial question: "How long does it take?"

"The least amount of time is six months."

As I hung up the phone, I realized there was another recognition seminar in Dallas — in almost exactly six months! I looked over my list of objectives to see what was necessary for me to be on stage in Dallas: 1) Make three presentations per week, which meant three evening presentations since I was teaching (I knew I could do that); 2) Find two qualified recruits per week, which meant I needed to ask at least eight or ten people per week. I thought I could do that, too.

If I didn't meet these two goals each week, I'd adjust my goals for the next week to make up for it. I transferred these ideas onto the planning sheets that we later adapted when we began teaching others the importance of goal setting in the "I CAN Way of Life."

Don and I set the goal together. He said, "Honey, I'll help you recruit people, I'll baby-sit, I'll do whatever I can." Mama was behind me too, but she used to worry about my driving the back country roads late at night, especially since I was pregnant with my second child.

One night at about midnight, I was driving home from a show when I heard a noise and felt the car swerve out of control. I managed to put on the brakes and steer the car off the road before I careened down the hill. I sat there thinking, *Here I am in the middle of the swamp in southern Georgia. I don't know how to change this tire. What am I going to do?*

Not too long after I asked myself that question, I saw lights coming up the hill toward me. As the headlights got closer, I realized it was a large truck. I wasn't sure whether or not I was glad that it stopped. Two men got out. Since there was a full moon that night, I could see that they were dirty from hauling logs and cutting trees.

"Oh, Lord," I prayed, "please protect me." I didn't have any protection — no Mace, gun, or even a fingernail file. "Could you gentlemen help me?" I asked the men when they walked over to my car. "I have a flat tire."

One of the men said, "Just a minute." He walked to the back of the car to look at the tire and then returned. "I think we can, Mrs. McCullough."

I couldn't believe that he'd called me by name. "How do you know who I am?" I asked.

"You were one of my favorite teachers when I was in high school. I've been out a couple of years now, but I never could have graduated without your help. Now, I can do something nice for you."

I was so thankful for that young man's coming home from a logging trip on that road at that particular time. You never know when something you do for someone is going to come back to repay you. The beautiful thing is that when these kindnesses are returned, they're often returned in larger proportions than we can imagine.

In six months I recruited and trained 56 people in the wonderful world of direct sales! I met with them each week to teach and motivate them. Our combined sales totals set new records for our company! The goal was mine, I was headed for Dallas!

What a wonderful convention! As I walked on stage wearing the suede suit I had seen in my mind so many times before I put it on my body, the entire crowd of seven thousand women cheered for me. I could see Don in the first row, smiling with pride in our accomplishments.

I had placed fourth out of 28,000 in recruiting, and the master of ceremonies presented me with a white gold ring encrusted with eight flawless diamonds. Then, as a surprise bonus, he gave me a solid gold, crown-shaped brooch embedded with a ruby.

I stood at center spotlight and accepted the cheers and bravos of the vast audience. I scanned the waves and waves of human faces and, in amazement, realized that a mere six months earlier I had been one of those faces in the crowd. Now, here I was on stage as one of the company's top ten! And all because of the motivation, goal-setting tips, and self-confidence I had gained from listening to Zig Ziglar and reading his book.

The same goal-setting steps that worked so well for me can help you tremendously too. Regardless of the area of your life in which you want to set and achieve goals, the same formula applies.

— THE SEVEN STEP FORMULA —

The first step in the goal-setting and achieving process is to *identify the goal*. This may seem somewhat elementary to you, but there are two key aspects of goal identification that many people overlook. First, the goal must be specific. A big home, a great deal of money, a profitable quarter or fiscal year, and helping others are not examples of goals. Real goals identified would be detailed and specific. A 3,000-square-foot home with four bedrooms, three baths, two stories, red brick — down to the wallpaper design and direction the doors open; $100,000 in savings; $500,000 in net profits; teaching three functionally illiterate adults to read — these are examples of *specific* goals.

Second, the goals must be stated positively *as if they were already fact*. "We enjoy living in a 3,000-square-foot home." "$100,000 in my savings account protects my family from sudden disaster." "$500,000 in net profits allows our company to grow and become even more profitable and helpful to others." "I feel good about me when I help others, so I enjoy teaching three functionally illiterate adults to read." This places the emphasis on the positive aspects of *goal achievement*.

The second step for goal achievement is to list the *personal benefits* that you will acquire upon achieving your goal. The key here is to be honest with yourself. If you list benefits to others, no matter how altruistic you may be, it becomes very difficult to sustain your personal motivation. Remember to remind yourself of the personal benefits of goal achievement.

I Can. You Can Too!

The third step in our seven-step formula is to *set a deadline* for achievement. When you establish a time line, you create a sense of urgency to take action on a daily basis. Your time line helps you to break your goal into bite-size pieces so that you aren't over-whelmed by the big goal. In *See You at the Top*, Zig talks about losing 37 pounds in 10 months. This breaks down to 3.7 pounds per month, .92 pounds per week, and 1.9 ounces per day.

The fourth step is to *identify the major obstacles* and mountains to climb. Goal achievement will not allow us to use the "ostrich philosophy" and stick our heads in the sand. We must identify our obstacles so we can plan to overcome them. Identifying a problem is 50-75 percent of solving it.

The fifth step is to *identify the skills or knowledge required* to reach the specific goal. You aren't required to be a walking encyclopedia; you don't have to know everything. A much more valuable skill is knowing where to find the information you need. By identifying what skills and knowledge are needed, you can now understand where to go for help.

The sixth step is to *identify the individuals, groups, companies, and organizations to work with* to reach your goal. As I stated in an earlier chapter, there are those who want to help you and are capable of helping you. Identify them and go to them. How often do you turn down people that ask you for help? Many people are flattered to be asked, so if you ask the right people, you get the proper help.

The seventh step in our goal achievement formula is to *develop a plan of action* to reach your specific goal. You cannot be too detailed here. Sometimes each step in your plan of action will need to be broken down into the seven-step formula — in effect, each step becomes a goal. This isn't always necessary, but if a goal is really important to you, no detail is too small. Plan your work and work your plan. Someone once said, "Proper prior planning prevents poor performance."

As a specific example of how to use the seven-step formula for goal-setting and achieving, I have included the worksheet I developed and used to plan my goal for success in direct sales.

— CONTINUED SUCCESS —

My success in direct sales continued to increase. I earned money, clothes, jewelry, perfume, trips, luggage, household items, and a variety of certificates, awards, and honors. My name and photo-graph appeared regularly in the Georgia newspapers and in our company's national magazine.

In the eyes of many people, I was both rich and famous. In 1976 I received an award from our company for the person who has most gone out of her way to help other people. The entire con-vention that year was awash with banners with my name on them and signs with my picture. The only thing missing was me! I missed the convention because I was pregnant with our third child, Jennifer. Bringing Jennifer into the world was the only other place I would rather have been.

The vice-president of our company called me from the convention and congratulated me on my new baby, and then added, "But, Mamie, dear, when we told you last year that we wanted you to be very productive this season, that isn't exactly what we had in mind."

Soon after Jennifer was born, I received a copy of our national magazine. My photo was prominent on page four, along with a full-page article that noted, in part:

GENERAL GOALS PROCEDURE CHART

Goal #1   Goal #2

STEP #1	IDENTIFY YOUR GOALS

STEP #2	MY BENEFITS FROM REACHING THIS GOAL

STEP #3	MAJOR OBSTACLES AND MOUNTAINS TO CLIMB TO REACH THIS GOAL

STEP #4	SKILLS OR KNOWLEDGE REQUIRED TO REACH THIS GOAL

STEP #5	INDIVIDUALS, GROUPS, COMPANIES & ORGANIZATIONS TO WORK WITH TO REACH THIS GOAL

STEP #6	PLAN OF ACTION TO REACH THIS GOAL

STEP #7	COMPLETION DATE

195

"Mamie is one of those people too good to be true! When she tells you something will be done, you can count on it! Mamie goes far beyond the expected; she does thoughtful and caring things for others that are totally unexpected. She is the epitome of thoughtfulness.

"In a company built on the Golden Rule, with so many caring people, it is difficult to single out someone as extraordinary. Even in this context, Mamie McCullough is special."

— MY DEFINITION OF RICH AND SUCCESSFUL —

As I travel around the country, people ask me if I'm rich, famous, and successful. I have to chuckle, but I usually reply by saying, "Oh, yes." I'm a success today because I have learned to get up every day and say, "Today I'm going to do my best." When I go to bed at night and say, "I have done my best today," then I know I'm a success. I'm successful because I have learned to control my life and not let circumstances control me.

Being rich, I discovered long ago, meant having things in your life that made you happy — children to love, a job that made you feel useful, and screens on your windows and paint on your house. Yes, I'm rich. I'm not monetarily wealthy, but I'm rich nevertheless. I am wealthy with good memories, and I'm content with the things I now have that I never had as a child. As I mentioned in an earlier chapter, it all comes down to *perspective*.

The saleswomen who worked with me in direct sales were in awe of all the attention I received from the national home office. One young housewife told me, "I'd be in seventh heaven if I could ever be rich and famous like you." I had to smile at that. The fact was, I had kept my perspective on things over the years. I was realistic enough to know that while I was well-known in my company, I certainly wasn't famous. No one hounded me for autographs, and to my students, I was just the lady who taught their class. But I had learned to set goals, plan for their attainment, and work like the dickens to reach them — and you can too!

— THE SEVEN STEP GOALS ACHIEVEMENT FORMULA —

Step 1:   Identify your goal.

        State it positively.

        State it as if it were a fact.

        State it in objectively measurable terms.

Step 2:   List your personal benefits from goal achievement.

        Be honest with yourself.

Step 3:   Set a deadline for achievement.

Step 4:   Identify the major obstacles and mountains to climb to reach your goal.

Step 5:   Identify the skills or knowledge required to reach your goal.

Step 6:   Identify the individuals, groups, companies, and organizations to work with to reach your goal.

Step 7:   Develop a specific plan of action to reach your goal.

— I CAN...AND *HERE'S HOW* YOU CAN TOO! —

1. "Bee a Goal-Setter." Memorize the seven steps in the goal-achieving formula.

2. We work for the things we really want in life. You must identify what you want, determine what you must invest to have it, and accept the responsibility for making the choice. Whether you want a housekeeper, success in business, a new job, or more free time, each has its price. Just remember what Zig Ziglar says, "You don't pay the price for success, you enjoy the benefits. You pay the price for failure!"

3. You must determine your personal definition of success. Whether it's a home with paint, shutters, and screen windows or the biggest home in your city, success is a personal choice. How will you know when you're successful? If you don't know where you're going, how will you know when you get there? Spend time alone and seek wise counsel to determine your definition of success.

4. Remember: What goes around, comes around. The kindnesses you show to others are like seeds sown to be harvested later. We aren't kind to others because we expect something in return, but when we show unselfish and unconditional love, it always comes back to us.

chapter 7

Bee a Good-Finder

*A*ndrew Carnegie was responsible for developing forty-three millionaires. When he was asked what attributes he looked for in order to make a millionaire, he replied, "I mine for gold." You often move tons of dirt to find a single ounce of gold, but you don't look for the dirt — you look for the gold. It's the same way in working with people. You must look for the gold, the good.

Are we looking for gold or looking for dirt? Do we really look for the best in our co-workers, children, or students? It has been said that parents and teachers give children eighteen negative remarks to one positive praise. As we see people we treat them, and as we treat them often they become.

My work with direct sales and my introduction to Zig Ziglar helped me stay motivated with my teaching. I was so motivated that I could hardly wait for each new fall semester to begin. But once classes started, I overheard students saying something I had never noticed before. They had a habit of saying, "I can't."

When I began to hear this, it occurred to me that children weren't taught to look for the good in themselves or others. Too often the cynical humor or the put-down was used, so unfortunately "I can't" was heard much too much.

So I said to them, "Students, you're always saying to me as a business teacher, 'Prove it to me'. As a business teacher, I have to prove debits and I have to prove credits. I want you to prove to me what an 'I can't' looks like. I want you to tell me the shape, size, and color of an 'I can't.'"

You can imagine the responses I got from junior high students. "Oh, Mrs. McCullough. That's impossible!"

"All right," I told them, "I want you to bring a tin can to class tomorrow." I didn't tell them what shape or size or kind to bring. I simply requested a tin can. That night I went home and cut out pictures of eyes from magazines.

Bringing in a can was probably the only homework assignment I ever gave that they all did. The next day I looked over the class-room and there were 32 students with 32 different sizes of tin cans. Some had Vienna sausage cans, some had soup cans, some had the gallon peach cans. Some of the boys had dragged the huge trash cans in from around the campus, but all 32 students had a can.

Never before had the individuality of group members so stood out to me. As I looked at that class, I was graphically reminded that each student is an individual who shouldn't be treated the same as everyone else, though they should all be treated firmly, fairly, and consistently. This obviously applies to groups of businessmen and women, church groups, and athletic teams as well. If we stop to consider, we will remember that every group consists of different types of individuals.

These students could hardly wait to see what I was going to do with those tin cans. I gave each one of them one of the pictures of eyes I had cut from the magazines, and I told them to paste the eyes onto their cans. When you put an eye on a can, what do you have? You have an "eye can." When you say it, the words come out, "I can." You can see, touch, and hold it, and you can describe this "I can" to someone else.

The students, however, still couldn't tell me the shape, size, or color of an "I can't." So I told my students, "Don't ever tell me 'I can't' until you can prove to me that there is such a thing." That little idea changed my students' attitudes. I told them not to say, "I can't get to school on time," "I can't get up earlier," or "I can't do my homework." I told them to tell me instead the real reason those things weren't getting done.

Soon after I explained this idea to my classes, our little Patti, who was three years old at the time, told me "I can't." I looked down at her and said, "Oh, darling, you must not say that. Mommie doesn't allow those words at school, and I won't allow them at home, either."

Then she looked up at me with her big blue eyes and told me the truth. "Mommie, I don't know how." And this has since become the philosophy at our home. *When you say "I can't," it either means "I won't" or "I don't know how."* We believe: If you don't know how, let me teach you; if you won't, let me spank you. I think everyone should have a choice, don't you? (As an aside, please remember: Never spank a child with your hand, and never leave a mark on the child. You spank to get attention; this is called punishment. *Discipline* comes from a Greek word which means "to learn." Punishment gets kids' attention so you can discipline, or teach, them.)

I Can. You Can Too!

One of the students explained the concept to her mother, who made her own "I can" and placed it in the window over her kitchen sink. It seems she hated to wash dishes, but with her visible reminder in the window she would constantly affirm: "I *can* wash these dishes. I *can* wash these dishes." Another child's father took an "I can" to his office and used it as a pencil holder and a constant reminder: "I *can* have a profitable quarter. I *can* have a profitable quarter."

HEARTITUDE:

Find the good

in all people

and all situations.

♡

Regardless of our daily activities, the "I can" reminder teaches us to look for the good in every situation, every day. An "I can" will teach us to "Bee a good-finder."

If you will write to me, I'll send you the label we now use for "I CANs." It fits a regular soup can perfectly: Mamie McCullough & Associates, 305 Spring Creek Village, Dallas, Texas 75248.

The "I Can" Philosophy

No one has ever seen an "I CAN'T" yet it has great meaning. . . it either means "I won't" or "I don't know how," both of which can be remedied with an "I CAN" attitude. We all need to be reminded of this regularly, so place this "label" on a #2 soup can and you have an "Eye Can." Put your pens and pencils in and keep it on your desk as your reminder to keep an "I CAN" attitude toward life!

The bees around the border are also symbols of the "I CAN" way of life. Scientists can prove that it is aerodynamically impossible for the bumble bee to fly - its body is too heavy and its wings too light to sustain flight. But the bumble bee chooses not to be influenced by science's negative viewpoint and flies anyway. When you look at the bee, think this thought - Yes, I believe I CAN BEE what I want to BEE!

Yes I Can

Bee What I

Want to Bee

Yes I CAN...

Yes YOU CAN, TOO!

Mamie McCullough's
The "I Can" Lady
305 Spring Creek Village
Dallas, TX 75248
(972) 437-5308

— HOW IT STARTED —

After reading Zig Ziglar's book, which was originally entitled *Biscuits, Fleas, and Pumphandles* (can you imagine selling the school board on using a book with that title?), I began to more fully live the concepts. *See You at the Top* (the present title) helped me realize that many of the rules I had seen in the classroom were negative. Everything was "Don't do this" and "Don't do that."

Too often as teachers (or managers, supervisors, spouses, parents), we force ourselves to look for the "bad" by establishing negative rules. Therefore, I decided that from the very first day of classes that year, I would instill positive attitudes in my students and help them be good-finders. I reasoned that if I stood at the door on the first day, smiled, spoke to every student, and shook their hand as they came in, I wouldn't be as apprehensive about teaching them. Nor would they be as apprehensive about learning from me.

I will never forget that first day. I stood and I smiled and I shook hands with every child. After everyone was settled in, I informed them we would all be good-finders, that we would have only positive things spoken in my classroom, and that we would have very few "Do not" rules. My main rule would be that we would always be positive.

I told them, "When you come in each morning, I want you to smile, look me in the eyes, and speak to me. When you answer questions, I'd like you to stand up. I want you to be positive. The Bible doesn't say that everything that happens is good; it says that all things work together for good. If we approach life expecting the best and *looking for the good*, we begin to understand what God's Book means."

I Can. You Can Too!

There was a young black student in my class named Charles who really took my words to heart. He was the epitome of the All-American football player. He was tall (taller even than me). He was big-muscled and had big hands. He was also one of the nicest and most pleasant young men I have ever taught. Charles had the prettiest white teeth you have ever seen. He would go to his seat, and every time I looked at him, he was always smiling. I thought, *Charles is really a neat kid.*

Now, as part of the school's career exploration program, I taught typing. In typing we trained students to sit up straight and to keep their elbows in, wrists and fingers curved, and eyes on the book. I was trying to instill all this into my junior high students. Well, I noticed that every time I would look back, Charles would be sitting there in the proper position, smiling. I know it must have been difficult for him to curve his large hands on the keys. But he had such a good attitude!

Then one day I heard something go, "Wham!" I turned around, and there was Charles. He didn't have a smile on his face anymore. In fact, he was angry. He had taken his hands and smashed them down on the typewriter keys, making the loud noise.

Quickly, I went back to him and said, "Charles, what's the matter?"

He said, "Mrs. McCullough, I can't find anything good about typing and smiling at the same time. I just can't do both!"

I laughed and told him, "You know, Charles, I tried that, and you're right. I couldn't smile and type at the same time, either."

The point I want to make is that often people — whether we are talking about our children, spouse, parents, co-workers, employees, or employers — will do exactly what we say, not necessarily what we mean. *Their* perception of what we're telling them and *our* perception are often two separate things. It's like the story of the three old men who were riding on a train from London to Wembley. When the train pulled into the station, one old man asked, "Is this Wembley?"

The old man next to him said, "No, you old fool, it's *Thursday.*"

At that, the third old man looked up and said, "So am I. Let's get off and get a drink."

Life is often like that little story. We know what we *think* we're teaching, but many times the real message isn't getting through. We must work diligently to be sure that our message is useful, understood, and carried out properly.

— AN INCREDIBLE CHALLENGE —

I was so delighted with the results I was getting from my students that I decided to develop an entire teaching format based on the motivation found in Zig Ziglar's book, combined with the child psychology lessons I had learned from my husband.

I began by putting a "Heartitude," which is a positive phrase like, "Do unto others as you would have them do unto you," on the chalkboard each day for the students' inspiration. Next, I established Fridays as "Mind-Building Day." On that day we would listen to motivational tapes, read motivational books, or discuss our experiences with each other. The results were phenomenal. My students improved their grades, showed greater respect for teachers, got along better with their parents, and took a stronger interest in their appearance.

That spring I made a long-distance call to Zig Ziglar's headquarters in Texas. In my traditional manner, just as I had done years ago with Dr. Guy Newman, I asked to speak to the person "in charge," and I was connected to Zig's office. I introduced myself and then stated boldly, "I want your permission to teach your book."

"Who to?"

"To my Central High School students."

Zig paused a moment. "But it's a book for salespeople," he said at last.

"As you have said, Mr. Ziglar, 'Everybody lives by selling something. These students of mine need to learn that lesson as early in life as possible. Besides, your material on positive attitude development and on building your self-image is exactly what the students need. So? How about it? Any objections to my using your philosophy and particularly *See You at the Top* in working to develop better students?"

As you might expect, Zig was excited about having his philosophy taught to students, but he was somewhat apprehensive about this "stranger" calling. By the time our conversation was over, however, I had persuaded him that I had something to offer. He said, "Well, Miss Mamie, with your successful experiences in business and education, and a husband with a degree in psychology, it seems to me that you would be perfect to develop the curriculum! Please keep me posted on your results!"

That fall I also realized that I needed to get to know my students better. I remember one of the girls in my business classes who always came to class looking tired and sluggish. Almost immediately after we had taken the roll, she would put her head down and fall asleep.

One day I asked her to stay after class. "Virginia," I said, "I must talk to you about something. Every day you go to sleep in class. Are you on some kind of medication?"

"No, Ma'am," she replied.

"Do you work after school?"

"No, Ma'am."

"Do you stay out late at night with a boyfriend?"

"No, Ma'am." Every question I asked her received the same reply.

Finally, I asked her straight out, "Virginia, why do you go to sleep in class? Are you that bored by my class?"

"No, Ma'am," she replied again, "I'm tired."

"But why are you tired?"

"Mrs. McCullough, I have nineteen brothers and sisters, and we have to take turns sleeping on the bed. We just have four rooms in the house, and two bedrooms. I go to sleep in your class because I'm tired."

In all the weeks when I'd wondered why Virginia didn't listen to me in class, I'd never thought of this situation. How could I teach these kids if I didn't understand their needs? The old adage is true: "No one teaches until somebody learns." Until I made some adjustments in my attitude toward Virginia and in her schedule, she would never learn anything.

I asked our principal if we could put her in a study hall or the library during the first two periods of the day so she could sleep. The librarian took an interest in Virginia and made sure she had something to eat. They became friends. In the next months,

Virginia not only stayed awake in class but also began losing weight she needed to lose because someone cared about her.

HEARTITUDE:

Do your job well

and like it...

Do your job poorly

and dislike it!

♡

I had to learn the lesson we were teaching in the "I can" course — to be a good-finder. Virginia didn't make it easy; I had to look past and overcome my original reservations. Do you have an employee who just isn't trying? A child with a poor attitude? A spouse who is at times indifferent? If so, let me issue you a challenge that will work in all environments.

Zig Ziglar's book, *Top Performance,** is without question the best management book on the market today. Whether you're trying to manage yourself or others, this book is must reading. Challenge #1 is to read *Top Performance*. In this exciting book, Zig issues the challenge to *catch them doing something right*. Challenge #2 is just that: Catch them (spouse, child, parent, brother or sister, co-worker, employee, employer) doing something right. Both of you will be glad you did.

— BACK TO HIGH SCHOOL —

The next year I returned to teaching at the high-school level. My title was Vocational Office Training Coordinator, which meant I not only taught business students, but also helped kids get jobs and then checked on them to make sure they were doing good work.

As I thought about doing this job, I wondered, What *would I*

* Zig Ziglar, *Top Performance* (Old Tappan, NJ: Fleming Revell, 1986).

want *if I* were interviewing someone? After all, I had been in the business world for ten years, so I had experience in hiring. Interviewers want to be good-finders. However, the interviewee often doesn't give them the opportunity. If I could help the students from an interviewer's perspective, then both could win.

First of all, I would want someone with a good attitude, someone who looked you straight in the eye and spoke up. This person should have nice manners, be friendly, and be courteous. All these attributes are very meaningful in customer relations. I decided that I had to teach my counselees these things, as well as how to apply for a job, how to speak clearly, fill out an application, and interview properly.

I used "Heartitudes" with these students. These are sayings like, "No one can make you feel inferior without your permission," and "Winners never quit and quitters never win." Each student would take some four-by-six inch cards inscribed with a "Heartitude" when he or she went to apply for a job. At the end of the interview, the student would say, "Here's one of the positive phrases we make in our school course where we learn the 'I CAN' way of life. I'd like to give this to you as a thank you for allowing me to interview with you. I've grown a little bit just by having this interview." The results were truly exciting! Listed here are some "Heartitudes" you can use.

— A ONE-MONTH SUPPLY OF DAILY HEARTITUDES —

Write each of these on a separate three-by-five-inch card and carry with you daily, referring to it often. *Results* are guaranteed.

1. You must first put something into your life before you can expect anything out of it. Zig Ziglar

2. Go out on the limb — that's where the fruit is. Will Rogers

3. They can conquer who believe they can. Virgil

4. It's not your aptitude but your attitude that determines your altitude. Jesse Jackson

5. No one can make you feel inferior without your consent. Eleanor Roosevelt

6. Take care to get what you like or you will be forced to like what you get. George Bernard Shaw

7. Inch by inch, anything's a cinch. Robert Schuller

8. You can't build a reputation on what you are going to do. Henry Ford

9. It's better to wear out than rust out. Dr. David Schwartz

10. Let everyone sweep in front of his own door, and the whole world will be clean. Goethe

11. A ship in harbor is safe, but that's not what ships are built for. Einstein

12. Keep away from people who belittle your ambitions. Small people do that, but the really great people make you feel that you too can become great. Mark Twain

13. If things go wrong, don't go with them. Roger Babson

14. Small opportunities are often the beginning of great enterprises. Demosthenes

15. We can do anything we want if we stick to it long enough. Helen Keller

16. Life is like the movies. We produce our own show. Mike Todd

17. Machines move mountains; but initiative moves people. L. Shield

18. Show me the person you honor and I will know what kind of person you are; for it shows me what your ideal person is and what kind of a person you long to be. Carlyle

19. The talent of success is nothing more than doing what you can do well, and doing well whatever you do. Longfellow

20. No person becomes rich unless he/she enriches others. D. Carnegie

21. Most locked doors are in your mind. Houdini

22. Your achievement can be no greater than your plans are sound. Unknown

23. Great minds have purposes; others simply have wishes. Washington Irving

24. The most I can do for my friend is simply to be his friend. Henry David Thoreau

25. Our friends are those who make us do what we can. Hamilton Wright Mabie

26. Be slow in choosing a friend, slower in changing. Ben Franklin

27. A friend is a present you give yourself. Robert Louis Stevenson

28. I have begun everything with the idea that I could succeed. Booker T. Washington

29. Determine that the thing can and shall be done and then we shall find the way. Abraham Lincoln

30. Giving up is the ultimate tragedy. Robert J. Donovan

31. As a man thinketh in his heart so is he. King Solomon

I began teaching the "I CAN" Way of Life at Central High School in Thomasville, Georgia. As the attitudes of the students in the "I CAN" classes improved, their grades improved in direct proportion. By the end of the first year, many students were claiming responsibility for their own actions! My principal, W. C. Childs, said that in his 37 years in education, he had never seen a course have a greater positive impact on students, teachers, and parents. Somewhere during this time, I began to see a larger picture. What if the "I CAN" Way of Life could be spread all over our great nation?!!!

— I CAN...AND *HERE'S HOW* YOU CAN TOO! —

1. "Bee a Good-Finder." Train yourself to look for the good that can result from all situations. In the Disney movie, *Pollyanna*, her friends and family were teasing her about this concept. One Sunday afternoon they were all discussing their lack of pleasure in attending a church where the preacher was very negative. "What can you find good about Sundays?" they asked Pollyanna. After a few thoughtful moments, she cheerfully replied, "Well, it's seven more days until Sunday comes again." You may have to search, but always look for the good. (And if you have a pastor who is more negative than positive, look for a new church.)

2. Keep your eyes and ears open! Who would have thought my life would have been so dramatically changed by a book called *Biscuits, Fleas, and Pumphandles*? Your answers may be disguised too. "When the student is ready, the teacher will appear."

3. There is no such thing as an "I Can't!" But you can create your own "Eye Can!"

4. Take time to know and understand those around you. Let others know you care — listen, listen, listen.

chapter 8

BEE POSITIVE

*T*he Greek root word for greeting means "joy." When someone says, "Hello, how are you?" how do you respond? Do you give joy? We choose how we respond, even if the other person's greeting is less than cordial. I tested this philosophy one time when I was in Wisconsin doing an "I CAN" Way of Life in-service program.

With briefcase in hand, I was waiting for the elevator in the hotel where I was staying. As the door opened, I faced several big fellows who were at the hotel for a heavy equipment convention. I thought, Oh, my goodness! I noticed they all had glasses in their hands. They had apparently just left the hospitality room and were weaving around before the elevator even started to move up.

I was debating whether to get on or not when one of the men reached over and pulled me in. I thought, I won't look at them, and maybe they'll leave me alone. I knew I had a problem when one of the guys said, "Hi-ya, Cutie." He was either drunk or had poor eyesight.

"Hello," I said.

Then one of them made the mistake of asking me, "How are you?"

I answered, "I'm supergood, but I'll get better."

I could see them looking at one another. I was wearing the bumblebee on my shoulder as I always do, so one of them asked me, "Do you know you have a bug on your shoulder?"

I thought to myself, I'm going to give them the works. I fumed around and they all lined up against the glass wall of the elevator. They had just given me plenty of room. "Aerodynamically," I told them, "a bumblebee can't fly. Its body is too heavy and its wings are too light. But the bumblebee doesn't know this, so he flies anyway. That means I can BEE anything I want to BEE."

Well, you could see them kind of blinking and looking around at one another. I was sure they were all wondering what had stepped on that elevator with them. By that time, we had reached the tenth floor, which was my destination, so as I made my exit I said, "Remember: I CAN...and you can too!"

I bet when they went home they told their wives and friends about that weird lady they met on the elevator! But I would rather people wonder than know for sure. It's so much fun to say, "I'm supergood, but I'll get better." I hope after reading this you will practice this phrase and use it. I respond this way all over the United States and have lots of fun.

In June of 1978, a scandal rocked the Thomas County School System. Rumors circulated throughout the county that our superintendent was misappropriating the school district's federal funds. More than 20 teachers turned in their resignations, and then on August 11, the principal of Central High School resigned. This was not a very "positive" time for the teachers and administrators of the system.

I Can. You Can Too!

More than 75 people applied for the job of principal of the high school. I knew several of them personally. The two obvious candidates were the vice principals of the high school who had been told they were being trained to assume the position someday in the future. Many of us thought one of them would be chosen. Some of the others who applied were coaches in our school system, veteran teachers who had earned graduate degrees in administration, or grade-school principals who were ready to move up the line.

On August 11, 1978, I was in my room at Central High School, washing down the walls so the room would be clean for the opening of school. The office secretary came to tell me that my housekeeper wanted me to call her. When I called, my housekeeper said, "The Board of Education is trying to get in touch with you. They want you to come to their office as soon as possible."

I returned the call to the Board, explaining to them that I was cleaning my room. "I have blue jeans on," I admitted.

"That's all right," Ed Cone, the new superintendent, said. "Come just as you are. We want to talk to you now."

When I arrived, the board members stood, and each was introduced to me.

After we sat down, Superintendent Cone said, "I understand, Mrs. McCullough, that you're known as the 'I CAN' Lady. What does that mean?"

"I CAN" means that you and I can do what we set our minds to do," I explained. "What other people say can't be done, those with an 'I CAN' attitude do anyway."

"Oh, really?" he said.

"Yes, sir. Folks said a woman over 30 shouldn't think about having children, but I didn't have my first one until I was 34, and I had my third one when I was 37. My husband and I wanted babies, so I had babies."

"And you continued to teach all those years?"

"Sure I did. I was back on the job two weeks after our last two babies were born. People told me you couldn't do that, either. But I did. And I also won a national contest in direct sales, taught Sunday school, and sponsored youth activities at the high school. But, more importantly, I could tell you dozens of stories of students who have adopted the 'I CAN' attitude and surprised themselves and their parents with their accomplishments.

"'I CAN' students from families where neither the parents nor their brothers or sisters had graduated from high school went on to graduate from college. These are students who overcame negative self-images and learned to believe in themselves, who translated the 'I CAN' principles into success in their business careers. I'm so proud of what the young men and women who have been involved in 'I CAN' have accomplished!"

"Impressive, impressive," said Mr. Cone, nodding his approval. "This must mean that you love children, both your own and the children you teach."

"Yes, sir," I said emphatically. "I truly believe that teaching is more than a job. Teaching is a mission. Every child has a future, and that future is going to be the direct result of that child's present. I want to make each one of my students' lives as positive today as possible. Then they can carry that good feeling about themselves into the future."

Around the table, the Board members winked at each other and flashed the thumbs-up sign. I had no idea what all that meant, but I was about to find out.

"Tell me, "said Mr. Cone, "would you be willing to do something of great importance for the children of Thomas County if you were asked to, Mrs. McCullough?"

It suddenly occurred to me that the Board was probably going to ask me to serve on a screening committee being set up to select a new principal for Central High. If I agreed to be a member, I would be committing myself to a lot of work. Still, the principal's position was an incredibly important job to fill, and getting as many opinions as possible would greatly help the selection process. I decided that if they needed my help, I would volunteer.

"Yes, Mr. Cone, I'm always ready to help the students of Thomas County, Georgia, in any way I can," I replied.

"Good," said Mr. Cone. "In that case, Mrs. McCullough, I'd like you to know that at a press conference set for eleven o'clock next Monday morning, I am going to announce that you have been appointed interim principal of Central High School."

The Board members gave me a round of applause, but I sat there transfixed. I was overwhelmed. I truly could not believe what I had just heard. *Me? Principal of Central High School? Me?*

In South Georgia, we used to have politics in education. I didn't know how people became principal. I had thought they had to have a winning football team to be principal. "But...but, Mr. Cone," I stammered. "There are many people more qualified." I named all six people who had told me they thought they might get the job. "Why me?"

"Two reasons, Mrs. McCullough," Ed Cone said. "First of all, we need someone who has a good attitude. We couldn't get anyone from any school system who could get along better with students, parents, and the community than you would. With all the rumors and headlines in the paper, we need someone who can stand up to close scrutiny. We believe you're a strong person, and we need that.

"Secondly, Mrs. McCullough, we have never heard you say an unkind word about anybody. You rarely go to the teachers' lounge, for instance."

I couldn't believe Superintendent Cone and the Board members knew that much about me. "How do y'all know that?" I said.

"We just know," he replied. "We've checked it out. We also know that your car is at school at 7:30 every morning and many times at night after everyone else is gone."

"We've seen those little Mind Builders in every store in town," another board member added. "In Maryland Fried Chicken. At Flowers Baking Company. In the bank."

That day I discovered that people do know what you're doing, even though you think you're working your fingers to the bone — grading papers, fixing bulletin boards, listening to kids' problems — without anyone appreciating what you're doing. And isn't that the way it is in all careers?

The executive spends the extra time at work with little or no recognition, and then "suddenly" everything begins to fall into place. The homemaker toils daily with the mundane activities that make life pleasant for her family but often go unnoticed, and "suddenly" she realizes that she has provided a positive home environment that pleases her and allows her family to grow too.

I Can. You Can Too!

Obviously, these things *don't* come about suddenly. There are many years of being positive that precede the "sudden success realizations."

Finally, I mentioned a necessary requirement I lacked. Surely, that would make the Board members understand that I wasn't the right person. "You realize that I'm not certified to be an administrator," I said.

"Then *get* certified," said Mr. Cone. "Go to night school and finish your master's degree this year. Remember? You don't know the meaning of 'I can't.' Let's see you put that to work." One by one, the other Board members added their own words of support and encouragement. Each asked me to accept the offer.

I rose from my chair. "Gentlemen, I'm deeply moved and greatly flattered by your offer. But I cannot answer you right now. I have two people I need to talk to. First of all, I want to talk to the Lord. I need to feel a peace about this. Second, I want to know what my husband thinks."

Don's office was 20 miles from the Board office, so I had plenty of opportunity to talk to the Lord on the way. I told Him the obvious: *Lord, I don't know how to be a principal.* Finally, I admitted, *If You're smart enough to make the world, You know who should be principal at Central High School. If You think this might be right, I need You to let me know. Help me to feel at peace with this decision or understand if it's part of Your plan for me.*

During the next minutes, a verse of Scripture came into my mind: "I can do all things through Christ who strengthens me."* I felt that the Lord was answering my doubts with one of the scriptural truths behind the "I CAN" philosophy.

*Philippians 4:13.

I could tell that Don was quite surprised to see me when I rushed into his office. Without even saying hi, I began to tell him about my meeting with the Board. When I finished, I sat down in the chair in front of his desk and asked, "So, what do you think, Honey?"

"How do you feel about it?" Don asked.

I looked at him and said, "Sweetheart, do me a favor. For this once, don't be a psychologist, just be a husband. Don't answer my questions with other questions, okay?"

"Do I do that?"

"There you go again," I said, and we both laughed.

Don sat back in his chair and thought a moment. Then he said, "You've often told me that the two greatest lessons you learned as a young woman were from Dr. Guy Newman and Mr. Herman Bennett. Dr. Newman said that people are brought to places for a reason, just as you were brought to Howard Payne College even though you didn't know why at the time."

I nodded. "That's true."

"Well," said Don, "maybe the reason you were brought to Thomas County, Georgia, was to become interim principal at Central High School during this rough time. If that's so, it would be wrong for you to deny your destiny. You remember, too, what Mr. Bennett taught you, right?"

I smiled and then repeated the phrase I had used so frequently during the past 20 years: "If you don't know how to do something, start."

"That's right," said Don. "And since you don't know much about being a principal, what do you think the best thing for you to do would be?"

"Get started," I said.

"Then tell the Board you'll take the job," he said.

The School Board had only one request. "Can you keep this quiet until Monday, Mrs. McCullough?"

"Can *y'all* keep it quiet 'til Monday?" I answered.

That weekend I had a wonderful time. On Saturday night I attended a big wedding in Thomasville. Everyone was talking about who would be principal, and many came up to me and said, "Mamie, you're a teacher. Who do you think?"

My answer was, "You know Ed Cone. I bet it's going to be a surprise." Nobody ever suspected that the principal would be a female, and no one guessed that I was the appointee.

That Monday morning, I sat in the back of the Board room with my tin can in my hand. The can I used then was a gallon can from the school lunchroom, with a big eye on it. The local television station was there with cameras. The reporters from the newspaper and radio were there too.

After all the preliminaries were over, one of the Board members moved that the Board appoint an interim principal for six months, until the new Board was elected. Another seconded the motion. Then Mr. Cone said, "We would like to submit the name of Mamie McCullough."

I could see people turn to other people with a look of surprise. "Who?" they seemed to be saying. "You've got to be kidding!" Then Mr. Cone asked me to come up front, and he repeated the reasons the Board had selected me.

Once the meeting was adjourned, the reporters surrounded me. I was busy the rest of that day until 4:00 in the afternoon, when I remembered Mr. Cone's last words of advice. "Go on up there, now, Mamie," he had said before he left the meeting, "and get your office set up, because school starts in ten days and you have 17 teachers to hire."

I walked very slowly into the principal's office until I saw the 12 bouquets of flowers sitting on the desk and every other surface. Three-fourths of those flowers were from my students, with a card saying, "We knew we would SEE YOU AT THE TOP, but we didn't know it was going to happen this soon."

— A SENSE OF DESTINY —

When I asked for a job description, the School Board told me, "You are in charge of the 'hill.'" The "hill" was our pet name for Central High School, because it's spread over a Georgia hill.

"You mean I can make the rules?" I had asked.

"Yes," Mr. Cone had replied. "But you've got to stand behind them once you make them."

I felt that this was my opportunity to apply the "I CAN" concepts to an entire school. I thought, *It's now or never. I'm going to have to walk the walk and talk the talk.* I'd been concerned about dress on campus, about smoking, and about some other basics. Now I had an opportunity to make a difference. I called a friend who was an attorney to make sure I could legally change policy, and then I began to formulate a brief list.

Nowadays, simplicity is sometimes frowned upon, but to me, one of the beauties of the "I CAN" philosophy is its simplicity. I created some basic, yet to some people's way of thinking, very different rules for a school in the 1970s. But before I could announce them, I wanted to discuss them with the faculty to get their input and suggestions. I brought all the faculty and staff personnel together and set down some guidelines.

"We're going to be old-fashioned at this school," I announced. "Besides the three R's, we're also going to teach the foundation stones of life: love, loyalty, honesty, trust, character, and integrity.

"Like Albert Einstein, I believe we teach in three ways: by example, by example, and by example. Since that's my belief, I'm going to expect each of you to walk and talk and teach and live in ways that constantly set good examples for our students.

"If you have problems, my door will always be open to you. There's one qualifier, however. You may never come to me with a problem unless you also have a suggested solution. I'm going to support your ideas, but I'm not going to do your thinking for you.

"Finally, you can expect to have me visit your classes from time to time. I plan to spend more hours in the field than I do behind a desk."

When my colleagues left that first meeting, the hallway was abuzz with commentary. Some was supportive, some was sarcastic, some was defensive. The rumors that circulated throughout the community in the next days were really amusing. Since I was one of only a very few women principals of an AAAA school of 1600-plus students, some said I would change the school colors to pink and white and that the pink panther was going to be the school mascot.

Soon after school began the last week in August, I held meetings with the girls in each class, and one of the vice principals met with the boys. I told them, "I think you ought to know what my expectations are, because I'm new at this." Then I talked to them about attitude, grades, attendance, manners, and dress. I simplified the dress code into one statement: "Cover up everything in the baseball 'strike zone,' the area from the shoulder to the kneecap."

When I told them about the no-smoking policy, I'm sure the students thought, *Ugh! She's really going to bear down on us!* The students had been allowed to smoke in a shaded area outside the building, but still on campus. Kids sat around on boxes and logs and smoked. Some of the teachers called this area "the cancer pit." I felt we were condoning smoking by allowing the students to smoke in that area. In announcing this policy, I told the students, "Look at the cigarette machines. It's illegal for minors to buy cigarettes. To me, that means that it must be illegal for them to smoke cigarettes."

A banner headline — NO SMOKING POLICY AT CENTRAL HIGH SCHOOL — appeared in the next day's paper. Of course, I got many, many telephone calls. Parents said, "We allow smoking at home. Why don't you allow it at school?"

My answer was always, "What you do at home is your responsibility. What I do with the children and the rules I make at school are my responsibility." I'm sure many of those parents thought I'd never be able to enforce that policy, but I did.

Of course, the students had to test my dress code policy. One day, my secretary burst into my office and disturbed a meeting I was having. "Oh, Mrs. McCullough," she cried, "there's a girl in the hall with just a halter top and short shorts on. What are you going to do about it?"

"Well, I don't know," I admitted, "but I'll talk to her after the meeting is over."

I waited quite awhile before I called the young lady into my office, because I really didn't know how to handle her. I finally decided that I couldn't procrastinate any longer, so I asked my secretary to call her out of class. She was a tall, big-busted young lady, whose figure made it even more noticeable that she was violating the dress code. I asked her name and then said, "Now, you know that our dress code is quite simple: cover up everything in the 'strike zone' from your shoulder to your kneecap."

"Yes, Maaaam," she answered with a slow, rather insolent drawl, "but this is all I had to wear."

"Now, Mary, I find that difficult to believe, because you wore other clothes all winter. You cannot come to school like this."

"Well, what are you going to do about it?" she asked defiantly.

"I'm not going to do anything about it. You are. You're the one who's not dressed properly."

"Welllll," she drawled, "we don't have a phone, and my mama can't bring me any more clothes, 'cause she's at work."

In the next few minutes we went back and forth between her excuses and my rebuttals. Finally, I said, "Mary, just a minute," and I walked over to the coffee pot to get a cup of coffee. That always gave me a few minutes to think.

As I looked up, I noticed a large, brown, paper dry cleaner's bag. Nowadays these bags are plastic, but back in the '70s, they were as solid as lunch bags (and made from the same kind of paper) and large enough to cover the freshly cleaned clothes — just perfect for covering the strike zone. "Mary, go out and ask my secretary for a pair of scissors," I said.

The young girl looked startled. She knew I had some strange plan. "What are you going to do?" she asked hesitantly.

"Never mind, just get the scissors."

When she returned, I enlarged the neck hole in the cleaner's bag so it would go over her head. I cut armholes out of each side, and then I turned to her and said, "Now, put this on."

"I ain't going to do it," she immediately cried.

"Yes, you are. I gave you a choice, and you gave me every reason why you couldn't get any other clothes. Now, I've made you a dress."

Mary put the dress on long enough to get out of the office and get help, I suspected. Not five minutes later, I saw her in the halls wearing a shirt that covered her strike zone.

— SIMPLE POSITIVE ALTERNATIVES —

I also felt that detention rules ought to be simple and to the point. Therefore, my rule was: If you're in trouble for being absent too many times or being tardy to class too often, you have two options. Either come in after school one hour every afternoon for a week, or be suspended for three days.

I knew that many of the kids who were put in detention hall were hurting the worst, because they came from difficult home situations. By making them spend an hour with me, I could control what happened during that time.

We listened to positive motivational tapes together. Sometimes we talked about "Heartitudes" and their application to students. Other times I had them write down their feelings about life and their teenage problems. Writing often helps us organize our thoughts and see problems differently and more positively.

Those students began to realize that it was a lot easier to obey the rules than to spend five afternoons with me, writing "Heartitudes" and learning positive attitudes. As a result, attendance and punctuality improved.

Let me encourage you to do some of these same things, regardless of your age or occupation:

1. Listen to tapes that help you maintain a positive attitude.

2. Form a support group of peers you trust and respect. Meet on a regular basis to discuss your areas of concern *and* your victories. Please remember to close these meetings by recalling the best thing that happened in your life since the last meeting. This will keep the meetings from deteriorating into gripe sessions and will help you all to focus on the positive.

3. Write out your feelings about life and your problems. This is very important. Problems seldom hold up under the harsh glare of reality as seen on paper. Writing out your thoughts and feelings helps you organize your ideas and keep everything in the proper perspective.

4. Use affirmations, "Heartitudes," Mind Builders — whatever you choose to call them. Let those positive power phrases lift your spirits.

You've heard it said a thousand times that example is the best teacher. Benjamin Franklin was one person who believed that old axiom. He felt that Philadelphia needed street lights, but knew that example would be more persuasive than argument. With this in mind, he devised a unique method of convincing his neighbors that Philadelphia should have those street lights. He hung a beautiful lantern on a long bracket outside his own door. He kept the lantern glass beautifully polished and the wick carefully trimmed.

Before long, Franklin's neighbors began placing lanterns outside their own doors. Soon the citizens of Philadelphia were ready to light their streets. Even Benjamin Franklin's most eloquent speeches were no match for the power or persuasiveness of his example.

That brings me to this question. How do you try to influence people? By intimidation? By steamrollering them into seeing your way? If so, you probably don't succeed too often. Even those times when you do, wreckage and hard feelings are probably left behind the successes.

I agree with Edgar A. Guest, who proclaimed, "I'd rather see a sermon than hear one any day." In short, doing and showing are more powerful than telling.

— WE'RE ALL TESTED —

About a month after school started, a couple of teachers rushed into my office one lunch time. "Mrs. McCullough," the first began, "two boys are fighting in the halls."

"What's your stand on fighting?" the other asked. Neither of them mentioned trying to stop the fight themselves, so I couldn't help but wonder if they, too, were testing me.

"My stand is, 'We don't fight on campus.' Bring them here and I'll handle them," I said, even though I had no experience in handling high-school boys who were fighting.

I made the boys wait in the secretary's office for quite a while. Finally, I called them in. After they'd told me their names, I asked,

"What's the problem?"

"He called me a name," one said, and the other immediately responded, "He called me a worse name." Of course, the verbal fighting began again immediately.

"Wait! Wait!" I shouted to get their attention. "We do not fight on Mrs. McCullough's campus. Do you boys understand that?"

They both agreed, said "Yes, Ma'am," and then turned to each other and began to fight again.

"Fellows,'" I shouted over their quarreling, "you heard me say that the rule is no fighting on campus. Now, I mean that. Sit down!" Then I contradicted myself and said, "No, stand up." An effective idea had just occurred to me. "I want you two to face each other."

The boys looked at me with questioning glances and then stood squarely in front of each other. "Now, I want you to get as close as you can to each other and look each other straight in the face." They moved dangerously close together; one's arm went out instinctively, either to fend off a blow or to initiate one. "I don't want you to touch," I warned.

Both boys turned and looked at me. "What are you going to make us do?" one of them asked.

"You have three options, boys. You can be suspended. You can come to my study hall after school every afternoon for a week. Or you can kiss and make up!"

It was amazing how fast that story got around school. By the time those two boys appeared in my study hall that afternoon, everyone knew why they were there. I didn't have to referee another fight after that.

I'm sure that the students thought, *We don't know what she might do next, so we'd better watch how we act.*

You see, I never posted or mimeographed a list of rules as many schools did in the '70s. If I had spent a lot of time with committees and the School Board, trying to get them to approve a list, I might still have been getting them approved at the end of the school year.

— A NEW CHALLENGE —

That fall was difficult. I had started school at Valdosta State College to get my certification as an administrator at the same time I began as principal of Central High School. Two nights a week, I drove one hundred miles round trip to attend classes. I stopped my work in direct sales, even though I knew I could make a great deal of money, because the "I CAN" philosophy was making a difference.

As a teacher, I had helped my classes. Now, as a principal, I was helping the entire school. With the number of evening meetings administrators must attend and my family responsibilities, it was a physical impossibility to continue in sales, so I reluctantly ended that phase of my direct sales career.

On September 15, I was leaving my office to attend a principal's meeting when I received a call from the local hospital. An intern said, "Mrs. McCullough, we need you to come to the hospital immediately. Your husband has been injured in a car accident."

Don was a pilot and had always said, "I'm not afraid of being hurt in a plane; it's those cars that get you." And sure enough, another driver had run a stop sign and crashed into Don's car as he was on his way to work that morning.

He was badly bruised and complaining of pain in his neck and back. The doctors kept him in the hospital for several weeks to test the extent of his injuries and to try to alleviate his pain. When he was released, he was told to recuperate in bed at home and wear a neck brace at all times.

Don was bedridden for many months. The kids went through measles and chicken pox. And my new job pulled me ten ways at once. Remarkably, however, I managed to gain my certification as an administrator.

By the time Christmas was past, I was exhausted. On December 28, I was sitting at the kitchen table, going over some of the materials Zig Ziglar had sent for me to edit, when the telephone rang. It was Zig calling to ask if I'd gone over the recent lessons. "What do you think?" he asked.

It was hard for me to respond. Finally I admitted, "Zig, you put these materials together, so I don't feel at liberty to say, 'I don't like this and this and this.' I don't know how to communicate that to you."

"Well," he said, "we can solve that. Come to Texas and communicate with me over my desk."

"Now wait, Zig. I'm just not a jet-setter," I replied. "I'm a mama. I've got to be here. Don's sick — "

"Why not ask him?" Zig interjected. "I'll pay for you to come to Texas for a day. It won't be that long."

Don did agree. "Your mother will help me look after the kids," he said.

The next day I was getting off the plane in Dallas. Zig hugged me as we met and looked me straight in the face. "Miss Mamie," he said, "I talked to the Lord this morning, and He told me that you were coming to work for me."

I couldn't believe what he was saying. Finally I responded, "I talked to Him too, and He didn't mention that."

"Maybe you'd better go back and talk to Him again," Zig suggested.

Later that day, as we sat in his office going over the suggested curriculum, Zig again brought up the subject of my joining the company. "Miss Mamie, you could make a greater impact on society if you would train other teachers to use this material."

"But I want to be in the classroom," I said. "I'm not staying in administration. I'll finish this year, and then I'm going back into the classroom."

"Miss Mamie, this would be just the time for you to make a big change. We've kidded about this for the last three years, but I need you. You're the 'mama rabbit' of this course; no one can teach other teachers to use the materials and concepts better than you can!"

Finally I said, "Zig, until something happens to my mother, I cannot move to Texas. I made a commitment when I went back to Georgia to stay and help my mama until she died."

"Bring her too," said Zig.

I laughed at that idea, but told Zig I would keep his offer in mind. The irony of this conversation is that just two weeks after his call, my mama died suddenly of a massive stroke.

Mama's funeral was not as painful for me as it might have been, knowing her life had been full, and her children had made sure that her latter years were comfortable. I knew I would miss Mama, but I drew comfort from the fact that she had lived to see me graduate from college, marry a good man, and have three fine children. She had died contented and, knowing that, I was also contented. We buried Mama next to Daddy, and they became partners in heaven just as they had been partners on earth.

When I called to tell Zig about her death, he replied, "Miss Mamie, is the Lord telling you something?" Don and I agreed to meet Zig and discuss his offer at his upcoming seminar in Montgomery, Alabama, at the beginning of February.

"I don't know exactly what I want you to do, Miss Mamie," Zig admitted during that meeting. "I do know I want you to talk to teachers, to visit with them over the phone, to write the course, and to do whatever it takes to help students and teachers become more positive." He never mentioned that I would be speaking to teachers all over the country. If he had, I never would have said yes. I had been too shy in college even to take a speech course.

As we talked further, Zig said, "I think I need both of you. Don, you're not only very articulate, but you're also methodical and can do all the proofing of materials and scheduling of seminars and workshops. There's a lot of things for both of you to do."

The beginning of that April in 1979, Don moved to Dallas to work for Zig and took the two small children, Brian and Jennifer, with him. They all stayed with his parents. Patti and I stayed in Thomasville until my responsibilities ended in June. The School Board offered to renew my contract, but I liked the idea of going back to Texas.

More than anything, I liked the idea of being able to work full-time with Don in a career we both saw as a mission. My vision of changing the classroom had become a reality. My dream of affecting an entire school had come to pass. And now, together, Don and I were on the threshold of making the dream of helping our nation become a reality.

— I CAN...AND *HERE'S HOW* YOU CAN TOO! —

1. "Bee Positive." Many must overcome negative conditioning and years of personal negativism, but the work is worth the reward.

2. Certification and qualification are entirely different. As we learned earlier, "When you don't know how to do something, start!"

3. Make sure you understand the rules you set and the reason for the rules. Then stand by what you believe.

4. We teach by example, by example, and by example. If you talk the talk, you must walk the walk.

5. Everyone has choices. We give choices to others, and we make choices ourselves. We can all *learn* to make positive choices, regardless of the situation.

6. Without a vision, the people will perish. Never let *anyone* steal your dream!

This is our earliest photo of Mama, Bertha Reddick Darlington, who was in her late 30's; Daddy, Mallory Darlington, was in his early 20's. On the left is the house I was born in; on the right is the house we lived in when daddy died. I was 3 when he passed away.

Below is a picture taken at my best friend Elizabeth Jones' 7th birthday party. We are both on the back row. Elizabeth is the second child from the left. I am the second child from the right. If you look closely, you can tell this picture was taken during a very difficult time in my life.

My fifth grade picture (age 10) doesn't look much different from my college freshman picture on the next page. With 9 children, we couldn't afford to buy school pictures every year, so I guess 5th grade was *my* year!

On the right is the oak tree I often sat under and wondered if I would ever know what was on the other side.

This is the Dixie school, and although today it is a private school, it looks much the same as when I was attending grades 1-12. In the front of the school is the "Hard Road." The picture was taken from Elizabeth Jones' front yard.

Below are the starters on our basketball team when I was in 10th grade. From the left to right, I am the second player. Notice my feet out in front of the others and my back against the wall so I wouldn't appear to be too tall. My sister Martha Ann is the fourth player, the sixth player is Elizabeth Jones.

That is my senior prom dress nearly covering the automobile I'm sitting on. In the background is the only picture of the house we grew up in. My mama paid $10 a month until she paid off the $250 it cost to purchase the home. On the right is my picture as a freshman at Howard Payne University.

Below to the left is the girl chosen "Most Pleasing To Behold" for two consecutive years at Howard Payne. Does she look like the Freshman above to you?

Eight years later mama sent the picture on the right to Don McCullough. The clock over my shoulder was a present from Don.

On the upper left Don McCullough and Mamie Darlington McCullough honeymooning. On the upper right is our first born, Patti, and her proud mama.

Below left, you will notice Patti eating cereal and ignoring the camera, Brian being fed and enjoying having his picture taken, and Jeniifer waiting to be born. The picture on the right was taken when I was Principal of Central High School in Thomasville, Georgia. We would all soon be on our way to Dallas, Texas, to work with Zig Ziglar.

This picture was taken 6 months before mama passed away. That's me on the left, Evelyn; Mama; Voncille; Mary Lou; Martha Ann; and June. Mama and me are in the upper inset.

Below left, three great kids lives are about to be dramatically changed. On the right is our family, one month before Don's death.

Top: Left to right; speaking for Zig Ziglar Corporation in the 80's; Mamie McCullough and Associates in the 90's; Teaching the Y.E.S. Seminar for as long as God allows.

Below, speaking at Howard Payne University when my dear friend Grace Pilot was awarded Honorary Doctorate. The inset photo is of Grace, the honoree. On May 17, 1997, the rolls are reversed. Grace speaks and I am honored as Dr. Mamie McCullough!

I wonder if Dr. Newman would have ever believed when handing me my college diploma (inset left) that there would be a building on campus named the "Mamie D. McCullough Athletic Complex?" Dr. Grace Pilot, the generous benefactor behind the building, and I are shown near the plaques identifying "The House That Friendship Built" (inset below).

Below, is the Darlington family reunion. We are standing in front of the First Baptist Church of Dixie, Georgia, which many of us helped to build and now attend.

Upper left: The three greatest kids ever, ready to enter a new phase of their lives.

Upper right, Patricia Lynn McCullogh now becomes Patrica McCullogh Wyman – Mrs. Matthew Wyman.

Lower left: My "silent giant", Herschel with the woman who loves him. On the lower right is our family today.

chapter 9

BEE A
GOOD
INFLUENCE

*O*ur influence is so important to those around us.
They watch us constantly to
make sure we walk the walk
and don't just talk the talk. I always tell teachers, "Don't tell
students not to smoke or drink or take drugs if you do these
things yourself. The students will always find out [the
grapevine in any school or office is notorious], and then they'll
never believe what you say again."

We must constantly ask ourselves if we're being good role models for our children. Brian asked me one day, "Mommy, why are
you mad at us?"

I replied, "I'm not mad. I just have a lot on my mind."

He retorted, "If you're not mad, why does your face look mad?"
Maybe I should have told my face I wasn't mad. How honest
children are! We're either a good or a bad influence every hour
of the day. Our influence is always showing. What are we teaching our children by our actions?

It isn't reasonable to say, "Now, Johnny, you tell the truth about
why you don't have your homework ready," and then when the
telephone rings and Johnny answers it and says, "It's for you,

Dad," we say, *"Tell them I'm not home." Actions speak louder than words. Our children are going to see our actions before they hear what we say. As Zig Ziglar says in **Raising Positive Kids in a Negative World**, "If we teach kids to lie for us, soon they will be lying to us."**

Zig Ziglar surprised us. When Don and I got to Dallas, we sat down with Zig to map out our plans for getting "I CAN" exposure to schools across the country. At that time, the only course the Zig Ziglar Corporation made available to schools was Zig's "Richer Life" course, and it was primarily used for business.

My first assignment was to write a teacher's guide and adapt student workbooks. The challenge and opportunity were great, but since Zig and I shared a common goal of getting "I CAN" into every school in the nation, I knew together we could help students (and teachers) be more positive about themselves and their schools.

Zig said to me, "Miss Mamie, I believe one of the great benefits that the 'I CAN' course will contribute to society is the impact it can have on teachers. There's no question that 'I CAN' has a phenomenal impact on students, and I believe that as teachers share the principles with their pupils, they'll learn to implement the concepts in their own lives."

"Yes," I replied, "there's no group in our society today that can positively — or negatively — influence our future more than educators. If this influential group grows by learning the 'I CAN' principles, and students grow by understanding the concepts, then we'll have helped *many* others become a good influence."

**Zig Ziglar, *Raising Positive Kids in a Negative World* (Nashville: Oliver-Nelson, 1985).

I Can. You Can Too!

My concept is that "I CAN" is a *way of life*. When we learn this positive outlook, we all can be a good influence on those around us. Since this philosophy is a way of life, the question that naturally follows is, how do we get others involved in "I CAN"?

The concept of the three-legged stool came up in our strategy discussions. The three legs of the stool symbolize the three areas we're influencing through "I CAN": students, teachers, and parents. If these three groups can "get on the same page" philosophically, many of the problems of our society can be solved.

Parents and teachers influence 100 percent of our future, the children. If those parents and teachers learn to think "I CAN," and children learn to think "I CAN," our future will really be bright!

Our dream seemed to be a great undertaking for an organization that, at the time, was made up of Zig, his wife Jean, Don, me, and three others. The Zig Ziglar Corporation was already overloaded from Zig's work with large companies.

"Have you ever exhibited at any of the educational conventions?" I asked Zig. He shook his head no. "I feel that we need to exhibit at selected conventions," I said. "That's where you reach the principals, superintendents, and teachers from all over the country. We can tell them about the course and show them results from other schools.

"We've got to make 'I CAN' a household word," I went on. "The Dallas Cowboys are on every cup, bumper sticker, and T-shirt across the country, so we also need a symbol that can be given to people."

In the next two weeks Don made arrangements for us to attend several national conventions, and we worked with a local firm to design a booth. We took the "I CAN" label I had developed in high school and used it for promotion.

At the same time, I began to enlarge the curriculum. First, I established goals for the "I CAN" program:

- To improve school climate and the morale of students and staff.

- To improve teacher attitudes and effectiveness.

- To prevent drug abuse in students, parents, and educators.

- To give students something to dream about so they do not have to go off into "dreamland" on drugs, alcohol, and other chemicals.

- To improve student behavior, achievement, and attendance.

Then I wrote a teacher's guide to the workbook Zig and I had been working on through the mail, and added instructional tools such as music, posters, and a citizenship book. We called our curriculum the "I CAN" course, and our motto became "Preparing Today's Youth for America's Tomorrows." I was billed as the "I CAN" Lady.

Once we began attending the conventions, we realized that few educators knew Zig Ziglar, since his outreach had been to businessmen. Don and I spent ten hours a day asking teachers and educators, "Have you ever heard of Zig Ziglar?" The usual answer was no. Don and I responded, "You should, because here's what his philosophy can do for your students."

I Can. You Can Too!

By the end of that summer, teachers and principals started finding out that I was on the staff, and they began saying, "We want you to come and tell our teachers how to motivate their students and how to have a good self-image."

Now, as I said earlier, I would never have accepted the job if I had known that it would include public speaking. But once I was on staff and we had moved the entire family to Dallas, I discovered that I would have to step up to the challenge of it.

The response to my informal talks to teachers and principals was so positive that Zig hired a public relations firm to book me with radio and television stations all across the country. I gave 50 speeches that first year and was interviewed by so many commentators and reporters that I lost count. Things were really rolling.

Even though I was traveling all around the country, I didn't feel guilty about being away from the children. Except for the conventions that we attended together, either Don or I was always home with the kids. I posted a weekly plan sheet on the refrigerator so the children would know the schedule for that week.

When I began this system in 1979, my children couldn't read. So we used color codes. They knew that Mama's color was green. I put a green star on the days that I would be away from home. Don's color was gold, so when he was to be away, the children looked for a gold star. When we were all going to be home, we placed a red star on the calendar. The children could look at the calendar and know when we were going to have some time together.

If you don't have time for your family, I don't think you're a success, regardless of what you accomplish. In fact, I think you're a loser. Because I love my family and because having a career is also important for me to have a balanced life, I plan time for both aspects. How can we be a good influence on someone we're never with?

Now, don't misunderstand. I was not at home every time I wanted to be or needed to be. However, I did set aside "protected" days on my schedule for family activities, recitals, school open house, basketball games, and other fun times. I regularly talked to the children about where I was going and why I was going there. At least once a year I took them on a speaking engagement with me, so they could observe first-hand what their mama was doing.

All our actions make value statements about what's really important to us. You may have your priorities listed as God, family, and company, but if you keep a time log of how you're spending your time for a single week, you'll see what your real priorities are. We spend our time on what's important to us. How are you spending your time?

One of the saddest comments I ever heard came from an eight-year-old boy. He told his friend his parents' divorce wasn't as bad as he had feared because he finally got his name on his dad's "To-Do" list. For the first time in eight years, the little boy actually was having regular time with his dad.

For those of you headed off on a guilt trip — forget it! Yesterday is a canceled check, and tomorrow is a promissory note. Today is the only ready cash you have to spend, so spend it wisely. If your family sees you working hard, that makes a positive value statement about the importance of good work habits. Just make sure you get your other priorities accounted for by spending time on each. This will enable you to *bee a good influence.*

— A HECTIC SCHEDULE —

While I was out of town, Don would work in the office during the day and care for the children at night. I don't want you to think he was a househusband and that since I traveled he made the beds and cooked meals. He did not!

In fact, Don was a practical housekeeper. His philosophy was, "Why should you make the bed when you're going to get back in it again that night?" He didn't like to cook, so we trained our children at an early age to get in the car whenever they got hungry. There are 6,000 great places to eat in Dallas, so why go hungry (and why should I have to do all the cooking)? I have healthy children, which proves you can raise kids on "public food!"

With that kind of laid-back view of life, you can imagine what Don and the kids did to the house whenever I would be gone for three to five days. They would color with crayons, water colors, instant chocolate pudding, and sometimes with shaving cream on large pieces of newsprint. They never cleaned anything up, because they planned to come back to it all later. Often, they never did return, and things just dried up on the newsprint. It was wonderful (for them). They had a great time.

One Friday night in the summer of 1979, I returned from a nine-day trip to Wisconsin, Indiana, and Michigan. I had spoken to schools and had TV, newspaper, and radio interviews. On the last day of the trip, I was in Indianapolis, Indiana. Months before, they had asked how many times I would be willing to speak in Indianapolis, and I had said, "As many times as you would like." Such a mistake!

I spoke in five different schools that day, and three of the buildings did not have air conditioning. Since I was wearing my new fall suit, you can imagine how hot I was.

I was still wet with perspiration when I arrived in Dallas that night, and I was so tired I could barely push down the accelerator in the car to drive home. Between the Dallas/Fort Worth airport and my home, I took off everything plausible: my shoes, tie, belt, jacket, and accessories. I took off everything I could without the truckers honking at me.

When I dragged myself through the back door that night, I was shocked at what I saw. The house looked as if someone had taken off the roof and dropped in a Texas cyclone for about 20 minutes, then taken out the cyclone and put the roof back on. I have never seen a bigger mess.

I couldn't find an empty chair to sit in. I couldn't find a light switch that wasn't covered with peanut butter. I couldn't even find a path amidst the clutter of toys, clothes, and dishes so that I could cross the room. I could have cried. Instead, I just turned off the light, kicked my way across the room, and went to bed.

At seven o'clock the next morning, I pulled myself out of bed and started to unearth "our" house. I had a housecoat that used to be a fuzzy blue but now was a slick gray after so many years of use. The matching slippers were frayed and scuffed, and that morning I could find only one. So I put it on and went barefoot on the left side. I didn't bother with make-up, because as active as I was going to be, I knew it would just drip off with the sweat anyway. My hair was still filled with the pink foamrubber curlers I had put in the night before.

Don and the kids were sleeping in. Messing up the house that badly had probably taken a lot out of them, so they needed the rest.

I began stumbling around the upstairs, picking up orphaned socks, crusts of pizza, scattered pieces of table games, treasure maps, ancient Aztec artifacts — anything and everything you could think of was piled there. I grabbed an armful of debris and started downstairs. On the way down, I passed a full-length mirror.

I stopped for a moment and looked at myself. The pink curlers were bobbing, the tired eyes were squinted, the old gray robe was flapping open, and my left house slipper was missing. I remember saying, "Well, no wonder you aren't getting anything done. Look at you. You're sick!"

At any rate, I kept working. I filled up two huge garbage bags with trash that had accumulated all week. Suddenly, I heard the garbage truck roll up to our house. *Hey! Wait!* I thought. *I want to get rid of these two bulky bags.*

I knew that if I tried to wake Don up, the truck would be long gone by the time he got downstairs. I looked so bad I really didn't want the garbage men to see me. *Oh, well,* I rationalized, *it'll only take a minute.* I went racing out the back door, my pink curlers flipping off in the wind and my one house shoe slapping on every other step. "Wait! Wait!" I yelled. "Am I too late?"

The man riding outside on the back of the truck yelled, "No, Lady, jump on!"

For me to be a good influence on those I come in contact with, I need to be at my best every day. So I learned a lesson. Ever since that day, I've made it a practice to get up early enough each morning (even on Saturdays) to get all my make-up on and to get fully dressed. Interestingly enough, I've discovered that I have to get up an extra 15 minutes earlier for each year I grow older. Five years from now, I won't even be going to bed!

Don and the three children got up around ten o'clock that day, and I fixed a big breakfast for everyone. "Oh wow, look," said Patti. "Clean plates."

That was another of Don's practices. Why wash those cereal bowls? We're all going to be right back here tomorrow morning anyway.

After breakfast Don went into his study and closed the door. I did 14 loads of laundry, vacuumed the house, ironed two dozen dresses, washed the dishes, and dusted the furniture. Around two o'clock, Don came out of his study and said he was going upstairs for a nap. The poor fella had been up since ten o'clock, so by now he was exhausted!

I was seeing red by this time. A nap! How could he? Men are so exasperating in their pragmatism. Don was tired, so he took a nap. I was tired, so I had a pity party. I sat down and bemoaned my fate in life. Now, in case you don't already understand, there are only two problems in having a pity party. First of all, you're the only one who comes, and second, no one serves refreshments.

I carried my pity party over to the next Sunday morning when we were up and getting ready for church. Caring for three small children is like organizing grasshoppers: It's almost impossible to do. I was having a lot of trouble, but Don was enjoying the morning paper. Jennifer was being especially squirmy. I believe the good Lord should furnish Velcro with all children under three years of age so that we could just "stick them on" and go about our business.

Understand, I never asked Don to help me. No, I was too busy having a pity party. All I had to say was, "Honey, will you help me with one of the children?" and he would have gladly obliged.

Finally, I decided I was going to have it out with Mr. Don

I Can. You Can Too!

McCullough this Sunday. When I got those three young'uns dressed, I took them into the garage. I strapped Jennifer into a car seat and set her on one side of the car hood. I strapped Brian into a car seat and set him in the car. Patti, my oldest, was running around the garage and getting dirty.

When Don, my big, tall husband, sauntered out the door, he had no idea what was lurking in the garage and waiting for him. When he spotted me, I pointed my finger right in his face, and I began to tap my toe angrily.

"Don McCullough, we have a problem!" I boomed, "and we're gonna settle this today. These children are as much your responsibility as they are mine, but every Sunday morning you don't do a thing to help me get them ready. I have to do everything! I give them baths, feed them, get them dressed, fill out their Sunday school envelopes, and strap them in the car. You never volunteer to do anything. I'm sick and tired of this, Mister! *We* have a problem."

Now Don was a wise man. A wise man is one who will let a woman run down before he tries to talk. After I had completely exhausted all my hot air, he looked at me and said, "Honey, *we* don't have a problem. *You're* the only one mad."

Well, if he thought I was mad before....

I bet it took me two days to cool down from that scene. But when I did, I realized he was right. I could have asked for help, but I didn't. I got mad instead. I could have explained how I felt or divided the jobs or made some suggestions. I didn't, though. I just had a pity party and then got mad.

Don's lesson wasn't wasted on me that day. When things go wrong, I always stop long enough to ask myself one basic question: "Who has the problem?" If the problem is mine, I try to resolve it. If the problem belongs to someone else, I either talk to him or her about solving the problem, or I steer clear of the situation. I'm not able to be a good influence on anyone if I can't control myself.

— "I CAN" SPREADS —

Our real success in the first two years of the "I CAN" program was in multiplying the Mamie McCulloughs. In Zig Ziglar's book, *See You at the Top*, Zig makes the statement, "Wouldn't it be nice if we had ten thousand Mamie McCulloughs across the country teaching these basic concepts of honesty, integrity, and positive attitudes in their schools?!"

Well, that's exactly what Don and I did. In the spring of 1980, we began a teacher-training program to help with in-service days, and we offered these sessions to schools across the country. We asked that everyone on the school staff be involved in the training, because I believe it takes the entire staff — bus drivers, janitors, lunchroom workers, and everyone else — to meet the needs of the students and make a school run smoothly.

Every person with whom we come in contact has an influence upon us, some positive and others negative. That's why *everyone* in your office, home, or school must be working together for common goals. The role of leadership is to influence others by example and word to work together.

In our schools, for example, quite a few of the students wouldn't have a nutritious meal if it weren't for the cooks in the kitchen. They wouldn't know what a clean bathroom looked like if it weren't for the janitors. When I was a principal, I discovered that

I Can. You Can Too!

I might be able to get by having five teachers absent on a given day, but if I didn't have five bus drivers and five lunchroom workers and janitors, I was in trouble. The entire staff forms the educational team, and this team creates our nation's future with its powerful influence.

During these in-service days, I challenged the entire staff, "If we look at just one student a week and say, 'Why doncha,' we'd make a world of difference. We have sales meetings at every company in the world except the school company. I believe that each member of your staff is a salesman, selling children on learning and education. I believe that you are the most influential group in our society because you are training tomorrow's leaders. Bee a good influence!"

After these in-service days, the teachers and principals took the "I CAN" program into their schools and positively influenced many students' lives.

— I CAN...AND *HERE'S HOW* YOU CAN TOO! —

1. "Bee a Good Influence." You influence others. Determine what impact you want to have, how you will go about exerting this influence, and why you want to do so. Remember: Every action is a value statement.

2. Set your priorities — God, family, and career — for a well-balanced life. Then make sure you're spending your time properly and wisely.

3. Evaluate your lifestyle, and include all family members to help with chores, as well as with fun times.

4. If you're the only one with a problem, maybe you are the problem.

5. Remember the wonderful people who were such a good influence in my life, the Jones family, the Newmans, the Bennetts? Each of us has the same opportunity to be a good influence in the lives of others.

chapter 10

BEE
PROFESSIONAL

*E*veryone can be a
professional. Prof-
essionalism is an attitude.
Business men and women
and even educators —
*maybe especially educators — can be pros in their careers. I wish
every teacher had business cards that read Professional Educator.
When parents come in for conferences, they could give them their
card. Even if the educators never used the cards, I believe they
should still have them! Educators are professionals, with or
without business cards or gold plaques on their desks or plush
carpeting in their offices.*

*Since we can all be professionals, we must first look the part,
which means being clean, neat, and color-coordinated. Fashion
is a look, not a price tag.*

*A lot of times people say to me, "You live in Dallas. You can go
to Neiman-Marcus, since you're not living on an educator's
salary." But my good friend Ethel Sexton and I enjoy buying
bargains at garage sales and resale shops. Don used to say I had
the wrong interpretation of a clearance sale. He said I took it
personally and tried my best to clear the store.*

The second aspect of being professional is looking and being organized. I believe school teachers ought to carry briefcases.

Just think of the appearance an elementary-school teacher makes as he or she gets out of the car in the morning, desperately clutching a pasteboard box that is "almost" covered with contact paper. Under the other arm are the papers he or she "almost" got graded. Does this teacher look professional? I don't think so. Most of this paraphernalia could be neatly stored in a briefcase.

The final aspect of being professional is to act professional. I believe it is very unprofessional to gossip or grumble. In fact, I believe employees should be terminated for gossiping.

You know what cured me of gossiping? Sitting in the teachers' lounge at school. The teachers' lounge is often the most negative room in the whole world, and I learned there that negativism breeds negativism. One teacher will remark, "Boy, Jimmy is on a tear today. Just wait until you get him next period!" When the colleague gets Jimmy next period, he or she is looking for Jimmy to misbehave. Poor Jimmy doesn't have a chance.

Someone said that on Judgment Day, St. Peter is going to line up everyone you ever talked about and make you repeat what you said to their faces. Now, that should get your attention!

Many coaches are professional educators. That statement may surprise those of you who have worked with nonprofessional educators who also coach, but I think you'll agree with me when I say that if all teachers had to demonstrate to the general public and parents what they had taught during the preceding week in a competition with another school, there would be a different attitude in our history, math, English, and science classrooms.

I Can. You Can Too!

Because of the pressure of public attention, many coaches become very professional in that they look the part, are organized, and treat their student athletes in a professional manner.

It's this same public attention that causes the nonprofessional to stand out so clearly.

One reason I'm so fond of coaches is that quite a few of the "I CAN" programs have begun with coaches who are interested in improving their players' morale and self-confidence. Jim Mercer, a physical education teacher in the Alvin Independent School District, a suburb of Houston, started the program there after he read Zig's book, *See You at the Top*, in 1979 and visited with me at our Dallas headquarters.

"Once I started using the 'I CAN' course, the athletes started showing up at 6:00 in the morning to lift weights and do extra workouts." Jim remembers, "They stayed late. One freshman who was big, fat, and slow came out for football that year. Everyone tended to write him off because they thought he would never amount to anything.

"That year he lost about forty pounds from lifting weights and working out, and everything that was left turned into muscle. The next year we had a kid who made All-District as a sophomore. By the time this boy was a senior, he had won just about every award you can imagine, including a football scholarship to Notre Dame."

Jim Mercer also used the "I CAN" program to inspire a mediocre basketball team. Every day before practice, he taught a lesson on self-image, attitudes, or achievement. That year his team won 24 games and lost 7. "It wasn't because we had good athletes, but because we had kids who had improved their self-image and believed in themselves," Jim says.

At the same time, Jim was also teaching an "I CAN" credit course once a week. One day one of his young students, Jeanie, approached him in the hallway. "You know this 'I CAN' stuff is a bunch of garbage," she began. "It doesn't work. You don't realize what it's like around my house."

Students began gathering around them as the girl continued to complain, so Jim suggested that they meet in his classroom after school. It would have been very easy for Jim to act unprofessionally in this situation. However, rather than getting upset, he chose the professional response by delaying the confrontation.

We can do the same thing in dealing with employees or even our spouse or children. Rather than emotionally reacting to a confrontational situation, take the emotion out by taking the discussion "off-line." Discuss your concerns in private, where no one will be embarrassed, and at a later time, when "cooler heads" can prevail.

That afternoon Jeanie told Jim about her problems. "Let me take a typical day in my life," she began. "I'll go home this afternoon, and my dad will arrive ten minutes later. As soon as he gets home, I become his slave. First, he wants a cold drink. Then he wants the channel changed on the television set.

"It's no better when Mom gets home," Jeanie continued. "She expects the table to be set before she arrives and the dinner started." The teenager also resented her older brother's distant attitude toward her and her younger brother's wandering off when she had to baby-sit him each afternoon.

After each individual problem, Jim interjected a little advice. "Next time your big brother's working on his car, why not go out and ask him something about his car? When you go to get your little brother, Bubba, put your arm around him and say, 'You know you're my only little brother, and you mean a lot to me. If something happens to you, I don't know what I would do. I want you to stay around the house so I know you're safe.' Then when you get back to the house, spend five minutes playing ball with him or doing something else together."

Jeanie promised to make a real effort to apply positive principles to her situation. The next few weeks of the "I CAN" course were devoted to relationships, so Jeanie was learning these principles again as she was working to apply them. Jim wasn't able to ask about her home life during that time, but he noticed her smiling at kids in the hallways for the first time. Then he saw her chatting with groups of other girls in the cafeteria.

Halfway through the semester, Jim found an opportunity to talk to Jeanie again. She told him what had happened after their first talk.

"I met my dad at the door with a cold drink and put the TV on for him. The first thing he said was, 'Okay, what do you want? What are you trying to get out of me?'

"'Nothing,' I replied. 'I'm doing these things because I love you.'"

Her dad's suspicious attitude continued for several weeks. Then he started asking her to bring two Cokes, and they began watching television together. Soon, he started telling her about his job as a policeman. "He just got promoted to sergeant," Jeanie said proudly.

Her mother was more difficult to reach. Jeanie began washing the dishes right after dinner rather than putting it off so her mother would nag her. The teenager helped with other household duties without being asked, but her mother never gave any sign that she realized what Jeanie was doing.

"One day Mom stayed to wash dishes with me," she remembered. "We started to talk about make-up and hair and shopping. We had a great time! We've become friends!"

Her older brother had almost responded too well to her inquiries about his car. "I know more about a car now than I've ever wanted to know," Jeanie said. "But now he asks me what's going on in my life. He's even going to ask Mom and Dad if we can double-date."

Jim didn't ask about Bubba until last, because Jeanie had expressed the most hostility toward him. But Jeanie smiled when Jim mentioned the little boy's name. "The first day I went down to the playground to bring him home, I reached out to put my arm around him, and of course, he ducked and tried to run away. When I finally caught up with him, I explained that I did care about him. That afternoon we spent five minutes playing ball, and now, every afternoon we do something together like baking cookies.

"Now, I have a real 'problem' with Bubba," she said with a laugh. "Everywhere I go, he's right behind me!"

Jeanie learned that the more she gave of herself to the members of her family, the more she received. Her self-image improved as her relations with her family became more loving. But Jim Mercer might never have been able to help Jeanie had he responded unprofessionally to her "attack" in the halls.

What he taught Jeanie was to respond in a professional manner to the negativity around her. Once she understood that the "pro" takes Personal Responsibility and Organizes their activities, she was better able to deal with her family.

I Can. You Can Too!

We can learn from Jim and Jeanie, and in our homes, businesses, and families, we can take Personal Responsibility and Organize our thoughts and deeds.

— FIFTEEN TIPS ON HOW TO BE
MORE PROFESSIONAL —

Listed below are fifteen specific steps to becoming *even more* professional than you are now, whatever your walk in life. I say even more, because if you weren't already a real pro, you wouldn't be this far along in this book. Remember: Professionals don't need to be told, but they don't mind being reminded.

1. BE ORDERLY The first requisite of discipline is order. A well-run office, home, or classroom sets the stage for orderly conduct.

2. BE NEAT. Maintain a neat office, work area, or classroom. Those working with you and for you should be impressed with the importance of neatness and cleanliness and should be given the responsibility of helping you keep your environment that way.

3. BE SPECIFIC. Establish set procedures. Having established policies will save your time and also prevent discontent among those around you.

4. BE RESONABLE. Whatever your individual standards may be, make sure they are reasonable, kept to a minimum, are well-understood by others, and fairly and consistently enforced. Don't ask others to do what you are not willing to do.

5. BE ON TIME. If you're only five minutes early, you're late!

6. BE MATURE BUT NOT "STUFFY." Be friendly always, but there's

a basic difference between friendliness and familiarity, for familiarity breeds contempt. You can think as others do and understand others without compromising your principles. In your work you are always the friendly person doing a professional job.

7. BE IN CONTROL. Insist at all times on respect for authority.

8. BE OBJECTIVE Don't be thin-skinned. Don't take undisciplined, aggressive behavior by others personally.

9. BE FREE FROM ARGUMENTS. Nothing is more demeaning than getting involved in arguments. You may discuss and explain, but you should never argue.

10. BE HONEST. No one is perfect; we're all human. Be big enough to admit errors.

11. BE HAPPY. Don't be afraid to show your sense of humor. Some incidents are funny, and you can't avoid them. Laugh *with* others and *at* yourself freely and naturally.

12. BE DISCERNING. Don't make an issue of everything. Sometimes it's best not to see every little misdemeanor that goes on. The important thing is to spot *real* trouble and to nip that in the bud before it becomes a major issue. Use discernment.

13. BE UNDERSTANDING. Please remember that love and respect are the two most unusual commodities we have in our society. The only way we can *get* them is by *giving* them away. This process starts with understanding.

14. BE WARM. Give warm fuzzies freely. Recognize unacceptable behavior for what it is: a symptom. The need for attention or affection, the expression of fear, resentment, or insecurity may

be the basic problems. By fulfilling these needs, you can show a person that he or she does not have to resort to unacceptable behavior to gain his or her ends.

15. BE COMPETENT. Generally speaking, it's an important part of your job to solve problems before they become unmanageable. When you need advice for handling a group or an individual, consult someone you respect, and don't wait too long. Get more training and increase your value to your organization.

When I think of professionalism, I think of Zig Ziglar's book, *Top Performance*. I heartily recommend it to anyone who can read. However, the real pro will especially benefit from studying this classic management (self and others) book carefully. I want to include ten "double-win" rules that Zig lists in that book, because pros look for the "double win."

— THE TEN "DOUBLE-WIN" RULES THAT LEAD TO TOP TEAM PERFORMANCE —

1. Remember that a smile is the most powerful social tool we have at our disposal.

2. Listening is the most neglected skill in business (or home) today. The person who listens controls the outcome of the discussion. Encourage others to talk, and then consciously remove any barriers to your good listening skills.

3. Talk in terms of the other person's interest. You'll find a "uniqueness" and "specialness" in every individual you meet. Others are interesting when discovered; check out the other person's point of view.

4. Ask questions you already know the answer to, and you'll get

to see the other person's perspective. Most ideas are more palatable if we discover them ourselves. People who truly care about others lead them down the "discovery path."

5. "What you are speaks so loudly that I can't hear what you say." Remember to model the behavior and attitude you want the other person to have.

6. Give assignments that allow you to express faith and confidence that the other person can successfully perform the task assigned.

7. Always make requests, never give orders. Saying "please" is always good manners.

8. Develop your ability to use the narrative story and the meaningful analogy. These are powerful teaching tools.

9. Always be respectful of others. Show your respect by being on time for meetings or letting others know why you must be late.

10. Return phone calls and letters immediately. There's no excuse for not doing so.

— I CAN...AND *HERE'S HOW* YOU CAN TOO —

1. "Bee Professional." People are drawn to positive, helpful, and professional people — whether teachers, students, parents, children, employees, or employers. Take Personal Responsibility and become Organized.

2. Remember: A wise teacher makes learning a joy, whether parent, manager, or teacher.

3. Each student, teacher, support staff, and parent is important to the growth of each child. Each manager, supervisor, and co-worker is important to each employee.

chapter 11

BEE
PREPARED

*H*ow can we prepare for the unexpected? In computer language you would say GIGO — "garbage in, garbage out." I believe GIGO means Good in, Good out, and the concept works on people as well as computers. The good helps you to be prepared for those times when you most need it.

One weekend the children wanted to visit their grandparents at the farm, but I was too tired to drive three and a half hours. As usual, they persisted. "Mama, please. Let's go to the farm. The goats are fixing to have babies, and we want to see the cups."

The children didn't mean china cups such as city dwellers store in lovely corner cupboards. They meant the mucus cups that animal babies have on their hooves when they're born to keep them from hurting their mothers. Soon after birth the babies lose these mucus cups, so we all knew that if we didn't go that weekend, we would miss one of the miracles of birth.

Finally I gave in. "I'll take you to the farm on the condition that you rest or read books quietly in the back seat of the car. I want to enjoy a nice quiet ride," I said.

They all agreed. When the children got into the car, Patti handed me a tape someone had given her as a birthday present. "Can we listen to this on the way to the farm?" she asked.

I agreed and put the tape on the dashboard. About 15 minutes later, I stopped to get gas and saw that the children were asleep. "It's too quiet!" I thought. I opened the tape and put it on. Half an hour later, I was wishing the children were awake so they could hear the lyrics. "Don't be complaining about your teacher and your looks," Evie Tournquist sang. "just be thankful." I decided to try to memorize the words so I could teach them to the kids.

Two hours later we reached Stephenville, our traditional stop to stretch and get something cool to drink. Now I had an excuse to wake the children. And when we got back in the car after the rest stop, I told Patti, "Your tape's great. Just listen to these songs." Soon all of us were singing along with Evie. "I thought you didn't know these songs," I said.

"We don't, Mama," Patti answered.

"You haven't heard this tape before?" I asked.

"No, Mama," the other two added.

"Then how come you know the words?"

The children had no idea. I had consciously tried to learn those 20 songs, but the kids knew them better than I did. Their subconscious minds, relaxed and asleep, had absorbed the words.

I suspect that our subconscious minds absorb much more than we realize. That's why I believe we must put the "good stuff" into our minds. We never know when we'll need that positive output.

Don and I had the responsibility of exhibiting at conventions to promote the "I CAN" course. This included the setting up of and working in the booth. We stood on concrete from eight to ten hours a day, answering questions about the "I CAN" Way of Life.

In September 1981 the school board for the state of Texas held its annual convention in San Antonio. We checked into a motel in the afternoon and then went over to the Convention Center to set up our booth. Around 4:30 p.m., we finished and decided to have an early dinner.

As we ate, Don talked energetically about different people he planned to meet at the convention and the sales techniques he planned to use to convince each person of the value of the "I CAN" course. One of Don's great strengths lay in his ability to prepare, down to the smallest detail. He was so excited!

When it came time for dessert, Don said no, but I had an outrageous piece of strawberry shortcake. "Don't be such a stick-in-the-mud," I chided Don. "Come on, have some shortcake."

Don smiled and patted his stomach. "When a man hits 46, he can't take it off as easily as he did at 26. No, thanks. I'll pass on the shortcake."

"You want to stroll down the walkway by the San Antonio River?" I asked.

"Sounds inviting," said Don, "but the travel today and working in that booth have made me a little tired. Let's go back to the motel and take a short nap. After that, we'll go for a walk, okay?"

I Can. You Can Too!

When I woke up from napping, it was just after 9:00 p.m. Don was awake and lying atop the other double bed with his back propped against two pillows. As he made plans and prepared for the future, he often made notes on a pad of yellow, legal-sized paper. He was busily writing as I gradually woke up.

"How ya doin'?" I asked, amidst a yawn and a stretch.

"Great!" said Don. "Tell me, what do you think of Wedgwood blue?"

"What do I think about *what*?" I asked.

"Wedgwood blue," he repeated. "As a new color for our bathroom at home. I think it would look great. You could color-coordinate some towels and a shower curtain to go with it."

"Sounds okay to me. But why are you worrying about the bathroom?"

"Not just the bathroom," said Don as he flipped forward through several pages he had been making notes on. "We should be re-decorating four or five rooms at home. I've got some good ideas too."

I sat up on the side of the bed. "Okay, Michelangelo, let's hear your master plan." Don was well-prepared, and I knew he would have some great ideas.

"Well, to begin with, I'd like us to repaint Brian's room with a nice shade of...."

Suddenly, Don stopped talking. I didn't understand at first what was happening. I looked at Don. His eyes rolled up into their sockets, his head jerked twice, and then he fell back against the propped pillows. One of his arms slipped over the side of the bed, and the pencil dropped from his fingers.

I had never seen anyone die before, but somehow I knew that Don was dead.

Quickly, I jumped to Don's side and shook him and called his name. It seemed the right thing to try. I picked up the telephone and dialed the front desk. "Send someone quickly, please. This is Mrs. McCullough in room 140. I think my husband is dead."

— ETERNAL SECURITY —

Two hospital ambulances arrived within minutes. Don was placed in one with the paramedics. I followed behind in the other ambulance, sitting up front next to the driver. Naturally, I was in a state of shock. I sat silently, thinking about what life would be like without Don McCullough.

We were rushed to the emergency room of San Antonio Baptist Hospital. Ironically, I was greeted by a Catholic priest who happened to be on voluntary duty as hospital chaplain that night.

"Are you Mrs. Don McCullough?" he asked.

"Yes," I answered.

"Do you know how serious this is?"

"Yes," I said, trying to keep my voice steady.

He motioned to a desk at the far end of the emergency room. "They have some papers for you to sign."

I went to the desk and the lady said, "These are for your husband to be admitted to the hospital. You do know it's very serious, don't you?"

"Yes," I replied. Everyone kept repeating this same question, but no one would admit that Don was dead. After I had filled out the papers, a nurse led me into the family room. The priest was waiting.

"Do you realize your husband is dead?"

"Yes, I do," I answered. The priest looked at me and waited for some response or reaction. I just said, "I know he's dead. I knew it immediately."

"But do you *understand* that your husband is dead?" the priest asked softly.

"Yes, I understand," I replied. I knew that he was wondering why I was so calm outwardly. Inwardly, I felt as if I were empty, groping for words that would not come.

When the priest asked if I wanted to make some calls, I phoned Don's parents. They couldn't believe what I was saying. Don hadn't been sick except for the pain of his back injury, for which he had continued to take medication. As I began talking to these dear people, I broke down and cried for the first time. The emotional impact of what had happened was slowly becoming a reality.

The next call I made was to Zig and Jean Ziglar. They were shocked and concerned about my welfare. They expressed the same concern for my being alone in San Antonio that Nana and Poppie had expressed, but I assured them I would be okay. They wouldn't be satisfied until I told them that Don and I had planned to spend the next night with some wonderful friends, Barbara and Walter Hailey of Hunt, Texas (near San Antonio).

Zig felt better because he and Walter were also close friends. Zig was sure (as I was) that when Barbara and Walter heard the news, they would come to San Antonio immediately. I called them and they left right away. Walter had a telephone in his car, so every few minutes he called me in the family room of the hospital to comfort me and check on my well-being.

As I waited for my friends to arrive, I thought about how glad I was that I had given my life to the Lord when I was twelve. Without the feeling of internal and eternal security that God was walking with me every step of the way, I would have never been able to accept Don's death so peacefully, nor would I have been able to deal with it with such control and dignity.

There's a well-known poem called "Footprints in the Sand" that tells how God walks beside us during good times and thus makes two sets of footprints on the sands of our lives. But sometimes we look back and see only one set of footprints. That's because God carries us during the difficult times.

How do you prepare for the unexpected? Is it possible to be ready when a tragedy of this magnitude occurs? That night at Baptist Hospital in San Antonio, God was carrying me. I give Him all the credit.

— FOOTPRINTS —

One night a man had a dream. He dreamed he was walking along the beach with the Lord. Across the sky flashed scenes from his life. For each scene, he noticed two sets of footprints in the sand: one belonging to him, and the other to the Lord.

When the last scene of his life flashed before him, he looked back to the footprints in the sand. He noticed that many times along the path of his life there was only one set of footprints. He also noticed that it happened at the very lowest and saddest times in his life.

This really bothered him and he questioned the Lord about it. "Lord, You said that once I decided to follow

You, You'd walk with me all the way. But I have noticed that during the most troublesome times in my life, there is only one set of footprints. I don't understand why when I needed You most You would leave me."

The Lord replied, "My son, My precious child, I love you and would never leave you. During your times of trial and suffering, when you see only one set of footprints, it was then that I carried you."

— FRIENDS ARRIVE —

When Barbara and Walter walked in the door, they put their arms around me. We stood there together awhile, each crying quietly and holding onto the others and our own memories of Don. How glad I was to have people I knew and loved to be with me during that long, dreadful night!

Death seemed to be closer to me than ever before. One minute, Don had been talking about redecorating the house. The next minute, he was dead, a quick and final moment in 46 years of life.

I knew that Don was with the Lord. What would happen if others I knew died so suddenly? I wondered. I looked over at the Haileys sitting across from me. "There's one question I've got to ask you, "I said. "I want to know if you're saved. Do you know Jesus as your Savior? Are you sure you're going to heaven if you die as suddenly as Don did?"

They smiled briefly and responded, "We surely are." That was a comfort and joy to me.

The Haileys stayed at the hospital all night with me. We prayed in the chapel, read the Bible, and tried to eat a meal together. They helped me get my belongings at the motel as well as arrange airplane reservations.

— A TIME FOR EVALUATION AND PREPARATION —

In the early hours of the morning, I went into the airport chapel by myself to think about what life was going to be like without Don. How would Don have coped with the situation if the tables had been turned? What if I were lying in a room down the hall and Don were waiting to sign papers to have my body transported to Dallas?

I knew that Don McCullough would still have been Don McCullough: patient, methodical, and organized. To honor his memory, I decided to approach my problems in the same way. I took out paper and pencil and began to think in writing.

I first thought about who I was, apart from Don. First, I was a mother with three healthy, beautiful children — God's greatest gifts to me. Next, I was the "I CAN" Lady. My message to folks for the past two years had been: It's not what happens to you in life, it's what you make of it. Now I had to decide whether I really meant what I had been saying or if that was all just a lot of propaganda.

HEARTITUDE:

It's not what happens to you, it's what you make of it.

♡

The decision was easy. I knew that I honestly believed in a strong self-image and positive life attitudes. I believed the verse in the Bible that says, "I can do all things through Christ who strengthens me." The Lord and I had walked through difficult times before;

we would walk that way again.

All, right then, Mamie, what can you find now that's positive about your life? I challenged myself. I began to write on that yellow pad, making lists just the way Don used to do. All my life I had said that every aspect of life was based on one's *perspective* of things. I had said that I was rich because I had a coat of paint on my house after growing up in a house without paint.

My intent was to list the positives and the negatives of my life. I never got to the negatives. Instead, I listed 19 positive things about my life. When I finished, I read the list straight through. Reading it did something special for me:

1. Naturally, my first concern is the welfare of our children. My mama had nine children to take care of when her husband died. I only have three children.

2. My mama had a second-grade education when her husband died. I have a high-school diploma, a bachelor's degree, and work toward a master's degree.

3. My mama had no place to live when her husband died. I own a beautiful, modern home in the suburbs of Dallas.

4. My mama had no clothes or appliances or money when her husband died. I have clothes, my house has many modern conveniences, and I have money in the bank.

5. I don't just have a job, but a mission. Any time you're helping others to achieve and grow and reach their potential, you're on a mission.

6. I work for a great company that believes strongly in the

family concept. I know the Zig Ziglar Corporation will have the children's and my best interests at heart.

My list went on and on. It was incredible how much better off I was than my mama had been. Don's death was going to be a deep, wrenching personal loss to me and the children, but we would go on, survive, and adjust to living without him. Once this revelation settled in on me, I felt in control of the situation.

As I continued to write down my thoughts and feelings, I reflected on those teachings that had meant so much to me. How could I be prepared to face the days, weeks, and months ahead of me? Only by using the information that I had gathered through my lifetime.

I thought about my mother's words: "You hear me out, Mamie Claire. There has never been a finer girl than you are, child. I raised you good, and you grew up good, and you *are* good." My mother was *there* during her lifetime to reinforce my belief in myself and to encourage me to *"be yourself"* — my best self. Now her memory was there to keep on reinforcing me.

I thought about Dr. Newman and Herman Bennett, who taught me to be a self-starter, and even my first husband who taught me to be a responder. Wonderful women like Mary Crowley and Mary Kay Ash flashed into my mind. These women were great role models, who taught me to set and work toward my goals while looking for the good in other people.

My work in education helped me understand the importance of being a *good influence* and a *professional*, and of *being positive*. Now Don's tragic death was teaching me to review what I had learned so that I could *be prepared* for the future.

I Can. You Can Too!

As you're reading these pages, let me encourage you *not* to wait until tragedy strikes to review and prepare for the events that will occur in your life. Every day you're preparing for tomorrow, whether you realize it or not. And if you will be open to God's leading in your life, you'll be thoroughly prepared for whatever comes your way.

Preparation is a cornerstone to every aspect of our lives. When I think of the great concert musicians who still spend many hours per day practicing their craft in preparation for even greater performances, I am truly overwhelmed.

Dr. W. A. Criswell, pastor for over 40 years at First Baptist Church in Dallas, Texas, who is one of the most knowledgeable men in the world about the Bible, still spends three to four hours every day studying God's Word. From these people we learn that a big part of preparation is *practice* and *study*. To be prepared, we must also practice and study.

Preparation demands that we give our complete concentration to the task at hand. Concentration allows us to give our best effort to our work and our play. Zig Ziglar is one of the best "Concentrators" I have ever observed. When he travels on business he "invests" his time very wisely. In airports and during flights he spends his time in research and writing.

On one trip, there was quite a commotion in the Denver airport as a group of teenage skiers were unloading and meeting friends. As I watched the activity, I noticed that Zig never looked up from what he was doing. Now *that's* concentration! He brings the same concentration to his free time with his family, devoting all his energy and attention to them, which makes his wife and children very happy (and as you might suspect, pleases Zig!).

Practice, study, concentration and *prayer* are all good tools to use in preparing to meet life's daily challenges. It was prayer that prepared me for what I had to do next.

— FACING THE CHILDREN —

The next morning, the Haileys took me to the airport to catch a plane home. As I boarded the jet, I talked with a flight attendant about losing Don. The crew did everything possible to comfort me. When I got off the plane in Dallas, Jean Ziglar, Nana and Poppie, and other friends were waiting for me.

I had requested that no one tell the children the news because I wanted to do that myself. My secretary at that time, Cindy Duce, and my friend and co-worker, Diane Connelly, had spent the night with the children. They met me at the back door of my home and told me, "They don't know yet."

The children rushed to me, as usual, and we exchanged kisses and bear hugs. Then I led them upstairs to a back bedroom. Patti, Brian, and Jennifer sat on the edge of the bed, and I pulled a chair up very close to them.

Patti said, "I can tell something's wrong, Mama. Where's Daddy? Did something happen to him?"

You know, the Bible says over and over that if we ask for wisdom and knowledge, we will receive it. That morning the Lord gave me wisdom. He helped me tell the children they would never see their father again on this earth.

"Children, let me explain something to you," I began. "Do you remember about two years ago when the Lord looked down and said, 'I need the best grandmama in the world? I need a grandmama who can sew, knit, and crochet. I need the one who makes the best homemade apple tarts and the best fried chicken there is.' Do you remember that?"

The two older children did. I went on, "Do you remember the day you saw her when her body was cold and hard because her spirit had gone to live with the Lord? The Lord only wants the best, and He took your grandmama because she was the best.

"Well, last night the Lord looked down and said, 'I need the best daddy. I need a daddy who is kind and gentle, a daddy who speaks Spanish and can fly airplanes, and a daddy who's smart. I need a daddy who knows how to be a good father and husband, a good brother, and a good son. I want a daddy who loves his children and loves the Lord.'" I reminded them of all the wonderful things that Don McCullough was. The children, of course, remembered all these things.

"The Lord came and got your daddy last night, children, and when you see him again, his body will be cold and hard because his spirit has gone to live with the Lord."

The children and I sat together and hugged each other and cried for a long time.

— I CAN...AND *HERE'S HOW* YOU CAN TOO! —

1. "Bee Prepared." It's not what happens to you in life that counts, it's what you make out of what happens to you. There's some good in all situations. Remember: "All things work together for good for those who love God."*

2. God has promised He will never leave us comfortless, but He never said we'd remain comfortable. Keep looking up when times are dark.

3. Friends are people who come to you in time of need. You don't have to ask them for help; they know and respond.

4. God never makes a mistake.

5. Practice, study, concentration, and prayer are keys to preparation.

*Romans 8:28.

chapter 12

BEE
CONSISTENT

I'm a very traditional person. I discovered years ago that to make a difference in my children's lives, I needed to do things on a consistent basis. I always tell teachers to establish their classroom rules on the first day of class. I also tell parents that they should have house rules, just as teachers have classroom rules. The boss who is a tyrant one day and your best buddy the next creates an office filled with paranoia and indecision.

We have rules in our home. Sometimes my children question them. "Are you sure this rule applies to Thursday and Friday, or is it just on Monday, Tuesday and Wednesday?" my kids seem to say.

I will never forget the Sunday morning Brian whined, "Do we gotta go to church?" Have you ever been in a hurry and everything went wrong? Well, that's what Sunday morning was for me when we first moved to Dallas. We moved from a town of 40,000, where we attended a church with 800 members, to the "big city," where our church had several thousand in Sunday school.

"What do you mean, son, 'Do we gotta go to church?'" I asked

him. *"You've been going to church since the day you were born. Why do you ask me if you've got to go now?"* We were standing in the downstairs hallway. I pointed to the stairs of our two-story home and said, *"Y'all sit down. I'm going to preach you a sermon."*

The children were three, four, and six at the time. They looked up at me with big eyes that asked, *"What is Mama going to do now?"* I said, *"Children, first of all, if it's Sunday, we go to church. Don't get up asking if you've got to go, because if it's Sunday, you've got to go. Do you understand that?"*

They nodded their heads yes.

Now, I'm a Baptist and all Baptist sermons either have three points or two points and a poem. I didn't know a poem, so I said, *"Third thing, don't ever ask for a motorcycle because you ain't gonna get it!"*

That simplified procedures at my house. My children get up and say, *"What day is it, Mama?"* If it's Sunday, they know we go to church. If it's Monday through Friday, they go to school.

Six years after I preached that little sermon, the children and I were taking a short trip and Brian said to me, *"Now Mama, I know I'm not gonna get it, but did you see the motorcycle in that window?"*

We need to be consistent in our rules, habits, and regulations. In this way, our children can learn there are specific things in life that we always do. You don't have to make a decision again every time. Decisions on how you're going to live and what you're going to do — whether you are going to be honest or dishonest, loyal or disloyal — are already made.

I Can. You Can Too!

The Bible says, "Train up a child in the way he should go, and when he is old he will not depart from it."* A consistent parent, teacher, or employer gives a child or employee steadfast criteria by which to judge his actions.

Once the children gained their composure, they amazed me by their perceptions of how the loss of their father was going to affect their lives. In fact, they each began to ask such logical and pragmatic questions. Don would have been proud of them.

Patti, who was eight, asked, "Mommy, who's going to help me have perfect attendance at church choir?" She had five years of perfect attendance because her daddy had always taken her to choir on Wednesday night.

I said, "I will, baby, or someone else will. I'll make sure of that."

The question Brian asked me that day, with tears streaming down his face, was, "Mama, who's going to be my soccer coach?"

I couldn't lie to the child. I couldn't tell him I would be his coach, because I don't understand athletics very well. Brian and his dad had shared this sport together. Since Don was reared on a foreign mission field, he had never had the opportunity to be involved in organized athletics. But his dream was to have a son who would be an athlete. When he was a professor in college, and after he entered the working world, he always had time for young people. He worked with the athletic program at the college and in the high schools.

I don't know if I had ever known Don happier than after we moved to Dallas and Brian started playing soccer. Don became his personal coach, even though he knew nothing about the game of soccer.

*Proverbs 22:6.

I looked at Brian and said, "Son, I think athletics are like the game of life. Those who hustle make it, and I want you to hustle. Just get out there and hustle and get the ball." That was all I knew to tell him.

Within an hour after I told Brian about his father, he went to soccer practice. He told his team, the North Dallas Chargers, that his father had gone to be with the Lord and that they would have to get another coach.

I promised Brian that morning that I would be at his games and I would be cheering for him. And I *was* at every practice and every game, shouting, "Get the ball, Brian! Get the ball!"

However, one day the coach called me over to the sideline and said, "Mrs. McCullough, I don't mean to embarrass you, but would you please quit telling Brian to get the ball. I've got Brian playing in a position where he's supposed to stay in one section and not play all over the field."

I promised to be less exuberant from then on. However, my "coaching" proves the point that you can do everything wrong but still succeed with the right attitude. The North Dallas Chargers were undefeated that year, and I take full credit.

Our youngest, Jennifer, asked, "Who will tuck me in when you're away, Mommy?" I honestly didn't know the answer, but that very day a woman I had never met before called me on the phone. She explained that she had been baby-sitting for a friend of mine, and they told her about Don's death. "I know this is early," she said, "but will you still be traveling now?"

I thought for a moment and then answered, "Yes." I had to travel to continue my work.

"Well, I would like to be your housekeeper if you plan to hire someone to live-in."

I couldn't believe that in a city the size of Dallas, this woman would be looking for a job and hear about Don's death from my friends. To me, this was another indication that God would provide for us.

— A QUESTION OF IDENTITY —

Earlier, I stated that security is an "inside" job. We must all take responsibility for our own security. For those people who really feel a love and concern for others, we can help them to develop their feelings of personal security by being consistent. Our repeated acts of love, concern, interest, direction, and listening will help children, spouse, co-workers, employees, and employers to have a feeling of confidence, at least as it relates to us and our relationship.

When we're consistent in our relationships, we help others know what to expect when dealing with us. Do friends or co-workers try to find out what kind of mood you're in before approaching you? This is an indicator of inconsistent behavior.

Children need consistency in their parental relationships in order to develop securities and grow in a positive direction emotionally. Don's death was going to require an extra measure of consistency on my part.

Another thing bothered Brian. He was concerned about his future identity. Later that day, we sat together in the swing on the back porch, talking and crying a little. Brian finally said, "Mommy, will I always be a McCullough boy, or are you going to change my name?" He told me about the children in his school who had their names changed and about the insecurity they seemed to feel.

The sun was shining down on us, but I shivered slightly. Still, I answered Brian quickly and firmly to dispel his fears. "Son, don't think for a minute that I'd ever change your name. You will always be a 'McCullough boy.'"

Not long after this, Brian asked me another question, "Mama, when are we going to be poor?"

"Poor?" I repeated. "What are you talking about?"

He replied, "Well, Mama, we know you don't work. Without someone working, we won't have any money."

I had learned, don't react, respond. I'm glad I learned that, because I was thinking, I work! *I travel more than one hundred thousand miles a year!* I *work* hard! Then I realized I had never gone home and told my children of any of the bad things that happened to me on the road. I concentrated on the positive aspects of my job. I guess I had made it sound so good that they thought I wasn't even working.

If I "blew my cool" because of his misunderstanding, I wouldn't be fostering further communications in this time when he needed so much for me to be consistent. If we're consistently calm when approached by our children (or anyone, really) no matter how wild the idea or question may be, we encourage them to approach us again.

— WHAT THEY DON'T KNOW —

I had never told the children about the emergency on the flight from Tulsa or the fire we had in the New Jersey motel. Those kinds of things didn't happen a lot, but they did happen. I always told them about the neat people I met, about the tasty apples from

New York, about the cactus and white sand of New Mexico, and about the ocean spray in California. Too many times, people dump all of life's garbage on their loved ones, and I had never wanted to be like that. I suppose they thought I was always out having fun.

I carefully explained to Brian that Daddy had worked as my partner at the Zig Ziglar Corporation and that I still had my job. I could tell that Brian wasn't completely convinced that I could be counted on as a wage earner. It just didn't seem logical to him, and I could understand why.

During our ten years of marriage, Don had been the head of the family. In that role he had handled our investments, bills, and other financial matters. The children had come to view him as the money person. On the Sunday before we buried Don, Brian went through a pile of Don's personal effects, which the hospital had given to me. He then came downstairs and told me, "Mama, I'm only going to give a little bit of my money to church today. I looked in Daddy's wallet, and it's empty."

I felt so sorry for Brian. I took time right then to explain to him that Daddy used credit cards and checks when he traveled and seldom carried much cash. This seemed to ease his mind a little, but it reminded me once more that children can perceive things in odd ways and that we must communicate with them regularly in order to explain away their fears. It took me several months to finally convince Brian that I was going to be able to care for the family financially.

— INTELLIGENT IGNORANCE —

I was doing some things correctly during this difficult time, without even being aware that my actions were psychologically sound. In looking back, I learned some lessons that I want to share with you.

During times of duress we need to maintain consistent and familiar routines. Whether our duress is caused by the death of a loved one, loss of a job, problems with a spouse or child — whatever causes our stress — consistency is a key to overcoming.

In difficult times, resist the temptation to retreat. Stay with your consistent routine of getting up at the same time every day, even if you feel there is no reason or purpose in making the effort. Go to work if you have a job, if you don't at least get active. Lying around the house in your bathrobe will add to your potential for depression.

Depression is more than a feeling of temporary sadness. It is sadness accompanied by a gloomy mindset, usually leading to mental "dullness" due to poor concentration and negative, pessimistic thinking patterns. Depression can last a few hours, several months, or years. It is not one simple, isolated emotion, but a culmination of many negative feelings.

The root words for depression mean "pushed or pressed down." When we feel ourselves getting into stress that might lead to depression, we must remember that the primary solution is consistency. *The problem is not the problem; the problem is my attitude about the problem!*

Dr. Les Carter, author of *Mind Over Emotion*,* says depression has reached epidemic proportions. At any given time, 15 to 20 percent of the American population is experiencing *some form* of depression—that's over 30 million people! Add to this the fact

*Les Carter, *Mind Over Emotion* (Grand Rapids: Baker Book House Co., 1985).

that there is so much misunderstanding about what this emotion is and how we can overcome it. The greater our understanding, the more we are able to deal with and "attack" this emotion.

As much as 85 percent of our depression (or extended sadness leading to depression) is caused by life's most stressful situations. Here's a list of the ten most common "stressors" of which we all need to be aware:

1. Loss of a loved one.

2. Loss of job.

3. Loss of a close friendship.

4. Loss of financial security.

5. Anger turned inward.

6. A blow to our self-esteem.

7. Improper perspective.

8. Improper priorities.

9. Fear of aging and dying.

10. Guilt — either true or false.

I want to share an example with which many of you will be able to identify. Recently, one of my associates at work had a tragedy in her life. She lost a close family member after twelve years of a beautiful relationship. Their cocker spaniel had to be put to sleep for humanitarian reasons.

Now before you say, "Wait a minute, Mamie. In one paragraph you're talking about the death of a spouse and shortly thereafter you are talking about losing a pet. How can you compare the two?" Before you rush into judgment, think with me for a moment.

No doubt there is a significant difference in the examples I'm using, but there is method in my madness. My associate was terribly hurt at having to have their family pet destroyed (those words sound so harsh to me), but those of you reading who would downplay the significance of this event are really adding to the problem.

If you don't take the time to face up to your stressors — if you think you must play the hero or heroine and not show your feelings — you are increasing the chance for your sadness to deteriorate into depression. Every *significant stressor* in life must be faced and dealt with. There are two steps in doing this.

—STEP ONE: RECOGNIZING POTENTIAL DEPRESSION—

There are some common indicators that you may be heading toward depression. You may recognize one or more of these in varying degrees, but remember these are *warning signs* to be used in solving the problem, not making it worse:

1. Becoming easily fatigued.

2. Loss of energy.

3. A feeling of hopelessness.

4. A lack of ability to enjoy normally pleasant events.

5. Overeating or loss of appetite.

6. Lowered sexual drive.

7. Indifference.

8. Irritability and the tendency to hold grudges.

9. Inconsistent concentration.

10. A tendency to be overly critical.

Now before you rush out to have yourself committed, remember that all of us experience one or more of these in varying degrees, *even in times of excellent mental health.* However, when the degree increases and patterns begin to form, you must recognize these as danger signals. That is where step two comes in.

— STEP TWO:
HOW YOU CAN OVERCOME
STRESSORS THAT MIGHT LEAD TO DEPRESSION —

1. A deep and abiding *faith in God* is the first and primary step in handling any and all types of stress.

2. Work to eliminate *bitterness* in your life. Bitterness is an insidious killer. It is devastating to the one who feels it, not to the one at whom it is directed.

3. Spend time daily getting close to your immediate family. Make your family a high priority and do everything possible to resolve family conflicts.

4. Spend time regularly having fun. Take life seriously, but don't take yourself so seriously that you can't laugh, smile, and enjoy life.

5. Set aside personal time daily. The most significant events in history have been preceded by moments of quiet solitude where those involved retreated to draw on the courage available to each of us. As Jesus did at Gethsemane, each of us must *make* and take the time to be still. You have a promise that you will never be given

more than you can bear, so if life seems unbearable, it may be because you haven't set aside personal time for renewal.

Please remember this: Failure is an event, not a person. When that message finally sank in, it was as if someone had turned on the lights for the first time.

— ONE OF MY MISTAKES —

One of the worst mistakes I made after Don died was not grieving his death properly. And frankly, this lack of grieving led to a state of depression lasting nearly five years. I made every mistake I have been warning you not to make, so I speak from experience. My failure to adequately grieve this terrible loss in the life of my children and myself was AN EVENT.

HEARTITUDE:

Failure is an event,

not a person.

♡

I AM A PERSON so I can overcome. After much research and some positive direction, I learned about the stages of grief:

1. Denial.

2. Anger turned outward.

3. Anger turned inward.

4. Genuine grief.

5. Resolution.

I learned the hard way that we must all go through each of these five steps. There is no skipping any of these. The road to mental health is a consistent observation of each of these, and many times we may need professional help in working through them. If so, don't be too proud to ask. The key is recovery, not how you get to that point.*

—OTHERS FEEL THE PAIN—

Don's death impacted people outside our family too. Don and I had worked together in the Zig Ziglar Corporation, and losing him was very hard on the entire company. On the Thursday after Don died, Cindy Duce, my secretary, called and said, "Mamie, we don't want you to worry about your speeches. We want you to feel free to take as much time as you need, and we're going to leave it up to you whether you want to go back on the road or not."

I asked her when was my next speech.

"Tuesday," she replied. "The Prestonwood Baptist Church Ladies' Group."

"I'll take that one," I said. "Call them and tell them they can count on me. Shirley Bobbitt, chairman of the Ladies' Group, asked me to speak more than a year ago, and I'm going ahead with it."

Five minutes after I hung up, Zig called me himself. "I truly appreciate your sense of loyalty to the company, Miss Mamie, but there's no need for you to rush back to work," he said. "If need be, I'll substitute for you myself."

Just to show you where my self-image was at the time, I replied, "Zig, you know those folks are expecting me. I don't want you to go up there and make that speech. They might be disappointed."

*Frank B. Minirth and Paul D. Meier, *Happiness Is a Choice* (Richardson, TX: Today Publishers, 1985).

Both Zig and I laughed then and for years afterward, because he is a great motivator and I respect his work tremendously.

The next Monday I went to see my attorney. He told me that everyone has a will — it's either your will or the state's. "Now, you'll have to prove that you're fit to have custody of the children," the attorney said. "You will have to be bonded, account for your income, and furnish other papers before you can have legal custody of the children or any of your other possessions."

I couldn't believe what I was hearing. I had carried and delivered those children. I had worked all these years to support them. The fear that my children could be put in homes, just as my relatives had suggested that the Darlington children might be put in an orphanage, was in the back of my mind from that day on.

I remembered a conversation between Don and me only a month before he died. We were coming home from the farm and passed a cemetery, which reminded me that we weren't prepared for death in our family. "Don, there are several things we really need to take care of," I had begun. "One is to decide where we wish to be buried if one of us passes away. Another — "

Don interrupted me: "Mamie, I don't want to discuss that." The tone of his voice kept me from going any further.

How I now wished we had. I often warn people when I speak: If you don't do anything else today or next week, have an attorney draft a will for you. You can have a simple will, which won't cost that much. But don't leave someone else to face the problems I encountered.

It's traumatic enough to lose a wife or husband, but not knowing whether or not your children or house are going to be taken from you doubles the pain and instability. The court didn't declare me the official guardian of my children until 1983.

The next day, Tuesday morning, eight days after Don's funeral, I woke up feeling empty. I was too exhausted to get out of bed, much less speak to the ladies of Prestonwood Baptist Church. I just knew that Don would want me to be there, however. So, as always, I decided to *start*.

Ironically, our best work is often done when we work despite the fact that we don't feel like it. Tchaikovsky, the composer, said, "Even the greatest geniuses have sometimes worked without inspiration. We must always work, and a self-respecting artist does not fold his hands on the pretext that he is not in the mood."

Jerry Clower says, "Every day I hit the floor on my knees and say, 'Lord, I was nothing, I am nothing, but with You I am everything, so crack Your whip.'" When we consistently approach the good and bad events with the same positive expectation, we *are* successful.

I reread a poem a friend of ours, Denzil Totman, wrote in Don's honor. (Denzil later copied the poem in calligraphy and had it framed so I could hang it in my office.) I read the poem "I CAN" over one final time before I left for Prestonwood Baptist Church: "If Don could speak, I'm sure he'd say, 'My work here on earth has stopped; but you keep pressing on, my love. I'll see you at the top.' "

— I CAN —

A lonely pathway down a lane,

That's filled with grief and sorrow.

You've never walked this way before,

But there's a bright tomorrow.

We do not understand the way

That God directs His own.

Although we cannot see ahead,

We never walk alone.

Death takes its toll on every man,

But death has not destroyed

The memories of those blessed years,

Together you've enjoyed.

If Don could speak, I'm sure he'd say,

My work here on earth has stopped;

But you keep pressing on, my love,

I'll see you at the top.

Now, just look up to God above,

By faith begin to sing:

"Oh, grave where is thy victory?

Oh, death, where is thy sting?"

Oh, yes, at times, it's hard to walk

The path that He's designed,

But just look back and you will see

The hills that you have climbed.

So on and ever upward,

Reaching goals each day.

Mark the victories you have won

By walking in His way.

Look up and thank Him through the tears,

As He reveals His plan.

And smiling, report to Him,

Lord, by thy grace...I CAN.

Denzil Totman

My sister, Mary, who was staying with me, accompanied me to the church. Church officials met us at the doors and led us to the pastor's office. Everyone there assured me that no one expected me to speak so soon after Don's death.

"I really feel that I can do it," I reassured them all. We drank a cup of coffee and talked until it was time to enter the church sanctuary, where the program was to be held.

As I walked down the aisle, I could see a question on the women's faces" *I don't believe she's able to do this.* But a miracle occurred that day, a witness that "all things are possible to him who believes."

I stood up straight, with my head held high. I've always said that I'm not a head speaker, I'm a heart speaker. If I ever spoke from my heart, it was that day. I told those ladies the story of my life, just as I had told many others. "It's not what happens to you that counts, it's what you make of it," I said over and over again. I was reaffirming the truth of that philosophy to myself as well as the 500 women in the audience.

Until that day, I had never realized how many times I referred to Don in my speeches. Each time I mentioned him, I felt a deep heartache and emptiness; yet, I kept going. I was even able to discuss the amusing parts of my life with the ladies.

I ended my talk by saying, "Last week when my husband passed away, I kept remembering how my one ambition as a child was to have a husband and children." I paused to look around at the women in the church. "Ladies, you don't realize how quickly that can be taken away from you. Please don't ever take your family for granted."

From that time on, I went back to my regular schedule, even though I didn't have much energy. Instead of work taking my mind off Don, I was continually reminded of him and how I missed him. Don was the detail person. He dotted the i's and crossed every t. He reviewed the material, supervised the manufacturing, coordinated the design and illustrations.

Who can I lean on? I wondered. But I knew that I could depend on the Lord. My business associates would help with my career, and close friends would help me outside the office. The real key was a complete trust in Jesus Christ as my Lord and Savior. Without *Him*, I could not have gone on. His consistency is eternal.

— PRESSING FORWARD TOWARD THE MARK —

I ached so badly that first year, I sometimes thought, *I don't want to motivate people.* I tried to push this thought away by reminding myself, *It's not what happens to you, it's what you make out of it*, and sometimes that worked.

I read motivational books and the Bible regularly to keep myself inspired. One particular verse of Scripture was very meaningful to me: "This is the day which the Lord has made; we will rejoice and be glad in it."* I knew after Don's death, as never before, that today might well be all we have.

One Wednesday night, the children and I were driving home from church and I started crying. Of course, when the kids saw me crying, they began to cry too. I pulled off Central Expressway and into the parking lot of a restaurant. Then I turned to the kids in the back seat. "I have to tell you something, children," I said. "I loved your daddy very, very much. And I miss him very, very much. There are times when my heart hurts so bad that I can't stand it and I have to cry.

"Sometimes, you're going to miss your daddy so much that you're going to have to cry too, but I don't need to cry when you do. So let's make a deal. If I need to cry, you will let Mommy cry. If you need to cry, I'll let you cry. Neither of us has to cry when the other does, because we'll all hurt for Daddy at different times and in different ways."

*Psalm 118:24.

— I CAN...AND *HERE'S HOW* YOU CAN TOO! —

1. "Bee Consistent." Maintaining a routine in times of difficulty can help you move beyond your trouble.

2. You can do everything wrong and succeed with the right mental attitude.

3. You don't have to "feel like it" to get the job done. Fulfill your obligations and commitments whenever possible.

4. The best thing to spend on children is T-I-M-E.

chapter 13

BEE LOVING AND CARING

*O*ne of the greatest hungers in America today is skin hunger. Mama used to tell me she always wanted a lap baby. I thought it was no big deal until my babies got too big to hold in my lap. Then I knew what she meant. There's something special about a little child sitting in your lap, being rocked by you. At those times, there is no way a mother can be depressed.

It's amazing what a touch can do. Everyone likes to be touched, whether they let on about it or not. In fact, doctors are actually giving "prescriptions" for hugs to older people. I don't mean you have to hug people until they turn a different color. A touch on the hand or shoulder or a warm handshake will work. Personally, I prefer a full-fledged hug.

How many times a day do you hug your children? A child who gets three hugs a day will be average. How far is average from greatness? Maybe just a touch away. If you really want to live it up, get 13 per day.

Cavett Robert, an outstanding speaker, says that 3 billion people on the face of the earth go to bed hungry, and 5 billion *people go to bed hungry — for attention. We forget how many lives we could positively influence by showing real love and concern to those around us.*

*When I think of real care, love, and concern, I think of the story Zig Ziglar tells in his book **Confessions of a Happy Christian**.*

A young businessman on his way home from work was seriously injured in a traffic accident and lost a lot of blood. His life hung in the balance, and a blood transfusion was desperately needed. However, he had a rare type of blood, and a donor could not be found.

Finally, someone suggested that his nine-year-old daughter Kathy might have the same type. Kathy's mother asked her if she would be willing to give her daddy some of her blood so that he might live. Kathy bit her lip, paused for a second and then agreed to do it.

Her blood was the same type, the transfusion was made, and the crisis passed. Little Kathy lay on the table after the transfusion, her body almost as white as the sheets she lay on. After a few minutes, her mother came into the room and told her that the doctor said it was all right for her to get up and go home.

*Kathy looked at her mother in shocked disbelief and said, "Mother, you mean I'm not going to die?" It's obvious that little Kathy thought she was laying down her life so that her father could live. ***

That kind of loving sacrifice is not a popular concept in our society today. But think about this: When the teacher stays late to work with the student who's behind in his or her work, isn't that a loving sacrifice? When a parent misses a special event

* Zig Ziglar, *Confessions of a Happy Christian* (New York: Pelican, 1982).

like a professional football, basketball, or baseball game to take the child to a school play, open house, or anything of seemingly less significance, isn't that a loving sacrifice? When an employer takes the time to listen, really listen (with his head and his heart) to what an employee is saying, isn't that a loving sacrifice?

There's one rule that will help you to master the "I Can. You Can Too!" philosophy completely: People don't care how much you know until they know how much you care — about them.

By January, 1986, my schedule seemed to be out of control. I spoke two to five times a week, many times five hours per day, a total of 8 to 16 times per month, and traveled to 34 states, often returning to the Dallas/Fort Worth airport late Friday nights. I rushed to my condominium, unpacked my travel clothes, repacked sports clothes for the weekend, and drove for three and one-half hours to the farm to be with the children.

I frequently wondered, *How can I keep myself motivated? How can I keep this exhausting schedule?* Participants in the "I CAN" course often ask me the same thing. Or they ask, "What suggestions can you give me for keeping my students (or employees or colleagues) inspired and motivated?"

I answer these people very candidly. I tell them that staying motivated takes daily effort. My mother used to say, "Every tub ought to sit on its own bottom." I didn't fully understand what she meant until I grew up and realized that each of us is responsible for his behavior, values, and attitudes. Staying motivated is a challenge. But it's worth the effort.

I also believe we need motivational symbols. I always wear a bumblebee on my shoulder as a symbol of the philosophy. As I've said before, the bumblebee is living proof of the ability to do the impossible. I always say I would rather have a bumblebee on my shoulder than a chip.

So far in this book I've discussed eleven "bees" to keep you motivated. These principles will help you to achieve the balance in your life that is so necessary to peace and contentment. They are as appropriate for parents as for teachers, as suitable for businessmen as for school administrators. The twelfth bee is the icing on the cake. Without this one, the others just won't be as effective as they might otherwise be. In other words, the twelfth bee is the glue that holds all the others together.

— THE BEE-ATTITUDES —

In Robert Schuller's book, *The Be-Happy Attitudes,* * he says that within arm's length there is always someone who needs our love and care. I heard another pastor put it this way: "Go out into the street today and walk up to the first person you see. Say to them, 'I heard about your problem.' Their response will probably be, 'Who told you?'" I believe everyone has needs and problems.

One of the people in our family who most needs love and care is Don's Aunt Anita, who was brain-damaged by scarlet fever at the age of five. Aunt Anita can remember dates, everybody's birthday, and everything that happened on a certain day in her past. But her sense of reasoning or judgment is gone. For instance, we have to tell her when to quit eating (although I'm not sure this is a criteria for mental retardation, since I know a lot of folks who don't know when to stop eating).

Aunt Anita has lived in a nursing home for many years, and since I joined the McCullough family, we have gone to see her at least

*Robert Schuller, *The Be-Happy Attitudes* (Waco. TX: Word. 1985).

once a month or when we visited the farm. One day after we had been to see Anita in the summer of 1985, the children asked me to sit on the back patio with them. "We need to talk to you," they said.

Brian began the discussion. "Mama," he said, "we don't like going to the nursing home."

"Oh," I replied, "why not?"

"Well, Mama, we go in the front door, and that fat lady wants to hug us. She is so big, we cannot even begin to reach around her."

"Yes, you're right, Brian," I said.

Jennifer took up their cause. "And, Mama, have you ever noticed how the home smells?"

I pretended to look perplexed. "Like what?" I asked.

"Like Mentholatum," she replied.

"Yes, I guess it does," I admitted. "What else don't you like?"

With this encouragement, the children mentioned a list of complaints, ending with, "Mama, the lady down the hall has whiskers, and when she kisses us, they stick to our faces."

Each time the children registered a complaint, I asked, "What else don't you like?" You see, before we can properly handle a problem, we must know *all* of the problem. We learn by asking questions. The intelligent salesman spends more time asking questions than talking about his product. The manager often asks questions he already knows the answers to so he can understand the employee's perspective.

"Your observations are correct 100 percent of the time," I finally answered after the kids had exhausted their list of complaints.

"However, we don't go to the home for us, but for Aunt Anita and the others. Some of those folks never have any visitors.

"And think of Aunt Anita," I continued. "She has never gotten to travel as you have. She can't play the piano as you can or sing in a choir. Children, I am asking you to go to the home for Aunt Anita and those folks, not for us. Think about that. We never choose our handicaps; therefore, we need to be kind and considerate."

As we walked back to the house, I wondered if I had totally confused them. Several weeks later, however, Aunt Anita was visiting the farm, and I overheard Jennifer ask Aunt Anita to rock her in our big, cane-backed Brumby rocker. I had never heard Jennifer make such a request before, so I listened for a few moments to see if Jennifer was trying to put into practice the suggestion I had made to her.

After a few comments back and forth, Jennifer asked Aunt Anita to sing to her. Anita has been to church all her life and knows every hymn in the Baptist hymnal, but few people ask her to sing them since she sings all the hymns on the same note. Jennifer, I saw, had really understood my message if she was willing to listen to Aunt Anita's rendition of "Amazing Grace"!

— THE PROOF —

That fall, the children suggested that we do a Christmas program for the home. Aunt Anita told everyone — the janitors, lunchroom workers, and any visitors to the home — that her niece and her children (meaning Aunt Anita's, not mine) were going to do the Christmas program. "The ones in the past have really been bad, Mamie," Aunt Anita confided to me. "I'm sure you can do better."

I soon learned why the previous programs had not been as well received as they might have been. The home didn't own a public address system. Most of the people at the home were hard of hearing, yet the home didn't have a P.A. I quickly offered to bring the proper equipment from Dallas.

Patti read the Christmas story from the Bible beautifully that day. I gave a very short speech about the meaning of Christmas, using an acrostic of Christmas. "C" is for Caring, "H" is for the Heart, "R" is for Rejoicing, "I" is for Interest in living life, "S" is for the Savior born on this day, "T" is for Thankfulness for life and family, "M" is for Memories of yesteryear and days like today, "A" is for the Attitude of Christ's love, and "S" is for Smile — it adds to our face value.

Brian and Jennifer sang several duets in their sweet, childish voices and then teamed up with our friend Sarah Baker, who had taught music at Howard Payne for nearly 20 years, for a rousing "We Wish You a Merry Christmas."

Aunt Anita cried through most of the program. Don's kids (her kids) were doing this for her and her friends at the home. Of the many pleasant memories of Christmas, 1985, the sweetest is our Christmas program for the Twilight Nursing Home.

The children and I learned again the truth in Zig Ziglar's saying, "You can have everything you want in life if you help enough other people get what they want."

In education, we sometimes are less than enthusiastic about our jobs. In fact, we sometimes make our jobs look so hard that we turn potential educators away. I found myself doing that the one day when my daughter Jennifer told me she wanted to be a teacher. Before I thought, I said, "Honey, you don't want to do that."

Do you know what she told me? "I would like to try it anyway."

Of course, I apologized to her and vowed never to say things like that again. We need to encourage good students to become good educators. We need to be enthusiastic about our jobs. Whether you're a manager, supervisor, CEO, or chief sanitation engineer, you must show real love and care for what you do.

When Jennifer was five, she wanted to be a teacher and a mother of eighteen children. Obviously, I had a little work to do with her (but I didn't begin until she learned to count).

— PERSONALLY SPEAKING —

In 1980, before my husband's death, Don and I went to Dr. Ken Cooper's Aerobic Clinic in Dallas. After my physical, Dr. Cooper, who is also a member of Prestonwood Baptist Church and a personal friend, looked at me and said, "I want to know what your schedule is."

I described the activities of the previous two weeks, and after I finished he asked, "Who do you think you are?"

"What do you mean?" I replied. I was a little taken aback by his attitude.

"There's no way you can have three children, be involved in church work, and travel the way you do, being gone three or four days a week. I'm going to give you some advice. First of all, for every day you're on the road, you need to stay home half a day. Secondly, you must exercise regularly."

I looked at him and replied, "Ken, how can I do that? You don't do it. Zig Ziglar doesn't do it."

"Yes, but we're not mothers with your responsibilities. You may think you're Superwoman; you may think you can, but you can't *always* do this. You're going to burn out."

I'm still learning to follow that first bit of advice, as you might guess from reading this book. But I did take his second suggestion seriously. You must jog, walk, swim, or be involved in some other regular activity to relieve pressure and help your body stay fit. Ken gave me a written report with an outline of things I could do to improve my health.

Finally I started to jog. I have changed from a positive thinker about the benefits of jogging to a positive believer who has put her thoughts into action. Physical fitness allows us the energy to show love and concern for those in our lives.

You leave your home daily to face a world of strangers in the best way possible, and when you come home at the end of the day to those you love, they deserve a motivated, enthusiastic, loving, and caring person as much as those strangers do. Exercise and time alone help us feel like being more loving.

— PERFECT DAY OF JOY —

Some of you may wonder about my life as a single parent. I am pleased to report that God allows me many days of joy! I believe we all should imagine what a perfect day of joy would be and then strive as often as possible to fulfill this vision. Just to show you how it's done, I want to share with you what my own perfect day of joy is like.

I plan my joy day for Saturdays so that everyone will be home. I rise early, put on my jogging outfit, go outside, and jog for half an hour. I am *not* a happy jogger. I run for my health. I jog alone and never worry about my safety. If you saw what I looked like when I first got out of bed, you would know why. Phyllis Diller and I are probably the only two women who can jog in a park and lower the crime rate.

After my jogging, I come back and read for half an hour or more as I cool down. I am committed to a program of continual study. Mark Twain once noted, "The man who can read but doesn't is no better off than the man who can't read." I read for fun and for study. I like the idea of beginning each day by making myself a little wiser than I was the day before.

After reading, I bathe and get dressed. I put on make-up and fix my hair. If the milkman or mailman comes to my door, I'm presentable. If neighbors or relatives or business associates come by unexpectedly, I'm ready. My motto is "Get up, make-up, go up!" I look as nice on Saturday for my children as I do during the week for other people.

Once I'm dressed and ready for the day, I work until noon. I handle the household chores that stack up during the week and take care of any "organizing" work that needs to be done to prepare for my travel during the coming week.

After lunch with the family, I usually take a short nap. The rest of the day I spend with my children. We may go to the zoo, play Monopoly, take a walk, tour a museum, go visit some good friends, or just sit on the porch swing and hug and talk. We really don't care, just as long as we are together.

Some of the most precious times my children have to remember are those things we do on Saturday afternoons. One summer Saturday afternoon we decided to make mud pies. I live on a creek where there is a lot to do, so I always have a yard full of children. That Saturday we had eight kids over at our place.

I Can. You Can Too!

I asked them, "Do ya'll want to make mud pies?"

"Yes, yes," they cried.

"All right, we'll make mud pies. You decorate them and I'll judge them and give ribbons for first, second, and third place." They were excited about doing that. They went out and made mud pies and decorated them. In the meantime, I went into the house and cut three blue ribbons, three red ribbons, and two yellow ribbons — eight ribbons for eight kids.

I went outside and there they were, proudly standing before their pies. "Patti" I said, "you get a blue ribbon. Jennifer, you get a blue one, and Brian, you get a blue one." Naturally, those were my three children getting first prizes.

One little boy asked, "Why did you give them first prize? That ain't fair!"

"What do you mean, 'It's not fair'?" I asked him.

He retorted, "That ain't fair. You're their mother, and you gave them first prize."

I looked at him and said, "Son, if you want to win first prize, you get your mama over here to judge."

Now folks, that child didn't speak to me for several months, but I feel that the one place a child should always win first prize is in his own yard. If you cannot be first place in your own yard, where can you be? Unconditional love is needed in every home, school, and community in our nation.

Twenty years from now, when my three children and I are sitting around the Thanksgiving table, someone is going to laugh and say, "Mama, remember the time we made mud pies and you let the three of us win first prize?" Then we'll all roar with laughter about that memory we made in 1985.

Life can be so very good. It's just all in what you make of what happens to you.

— SOME FINAL THOUGHTS —

As I was putting the finishing touches on this book, I had some important lessons reinforced in my own life. These lessons pointed out to me that we don't "go" through life, we "grow" through it. And while I've completed this book, I haven't completed my life. By the time you actually read these words, I sincerely believe that God will have taught me even more. Like you, I'm learning daily.

I recently learned that the "I CAN" Lady is not Superwoman. I simply used poor judgment and pushed myself to the point of exhaustion. After taking two weeks off for rest and relaxation, I attended seminars on stress reduction, exercise, and nutrition. Let me urge you to be smarter than I was and not wait until you're "too pooped to pop" and plan your work time.

Please — get involved in an exercise program (under a doctor's direction) and learn about proper nutrition. The Pritikin Longevity Center in Santa Monica, California, and Philadelphia, Pennsylvania, or the Cooper Wellness Center in Dallas, Texas, are excellent sources for the type of information I'm talking about.

For those of you praying for my children and for me, thank you! You will be proud to know that Patti, Brian, and Jennifer are the happiest, most well-adjusted, warmest, most loving, kindest, and most sensitive children God ever put on this earth. Now, I know you'll recognize that these obvious statements of truth are coming from a completely unbiased, nonprejudicial, and objective observer. I do love my children!

Once the famous author Rudyard Kipling was interviewed by a reporter who stated: "Mr. Kipling, I understand that you receive as much as $100 per word for some of your writings."

Mr. Kipling replied, "Yes, I do."

The reporter took out a crisp, new $100 bill and said, "Would you please give me one of your $100 words for this $100 bill?"

Mr. Kipling paused, took the $100 bill, smiled, said "Thanks," and walked away.

As we "walk away" from each other, I want you to know how much I appreciate your reading these words. There may not be any worth $100, but if you've learned half as much from reading this book as I've learned in writing it, then the time investment we've both made is worthwhile.

— A HAPPY "BEGINNING" —

As I bring this book to a close*, I want to give you some *really* exciting news. We do have a wonderful and loving God. From the day I began this project until today, *many* things have happened in my life. And in the last few months I have been *blessed*.

Today my family and I live in Dallas, Texas, and enjoy God's blessings at Prestonwood Baptist Church. Spiritually, we are extremely happy.

The children like Dallas, and my schedule is well-coordinated to allow the proper balance between travel and the vitally important home life we need. So my family life is fantastic.

The "I CAN" Way of Life, which has been my mission and my

career, has made more progress in the last six months than it did in its first six years of existence. We *are* changing lives. My career makes me happy and helps others too!

And finally, a special thank you to you. If you've "hung in there" long enough to get to this point, you know me about as well as anyone on the face of this earth...and I like that! You see, if you know me, that means we are brothers and sisters in life's journey. If you know Jesus Christ, then we will be brothers and sisters for eternity. Now, *that's* a comforting thought.

*This is the way the book closed in 1987.

I Can. You Can Too!

— I CAN...AND *HERE'S HOW* YOU CAN TOO! —

1. "Bee There." You are the best person for the job or task. You took the job! Being there every day possible is vitally important. There's really no substitute for you.

2. "Bee Yourself." Let people see the real you. Adults and children benefit when you have positive self-esteem; you know yourself, they can know you, and understanding is enhanced. Self-esteem is fundamental to basic happiness.

3. "Bee a Self-Starter." Do it now! When you don't know how to do something, *start*. Beware of the paralysis of analysis. Be a person of *action*.

4. "Bee a Responder." Refuse to react negatively! Take the positive approach and respond positively. Remember, *the choice is yours*.

5. "Bee a Goal-Setter." Set goals in seven areas for the balanced life — physical, mental, spiritual, family, financial, career, and social — and review them often. Goals are your road map to success.

6. "Bee a Good-Finder." Look for the good in others. An ounce of gold is covered by tons of dirt, but we don't look for the dirt. Find the gold in people.

7. "Bee Positive." Good books, good people, and good cassette tapes help us put good, clean, pure, powerful, and positive thoughts into our minds.

8. "Bee a Good Influence." People form attitudes about others based on your actions. Take responsibility for your actions on a daily basis.

9. "Bee Professional." "A professional makes the job look easy." How do others perceive you and your job? Look, act, and live like a professional.

10. "Bee Prepared." Remember the five P's: "Proper Planning Prevents Poor Performance!" Organize and prepare for work and family. Strive for balance between the two.

11. "Bee Consistent." Consistency in discipline and attitude is extremely important. Do others know what to expect from you?

12. "Bee Loving and Caring." People don't care how much you know until they know how much you care — about them. Show others you care!

chapter 14

TEN
YEARS
LATER

Today is the best day of my life because I decided it would be. Now if these words sound familiar to you, they should! I started writing *I Can. You Can Too!* ten years ago with those same words. And guess what?! Today *is* the best day of my life! Today is the best day because I decided it would be *then —* *and now! I Can. You Can Too!* was written to help you be able to get up in the morning and *choose* to make *today* the best day of your life.

The 10th Anniversary Edition of *I Can. You Can Too!* is written to offer perspective on the lessons shared in the first edition of the book and also on new lessons to be learned. And if I have learned anything in the past decade it is this: Our basic freedom is the freedom of choice.

At the most fundamental level of our lives, we make the decisions that will determine what kind of day, and ultimately the life, we are going to lead. With every choice comes a consequence. Mary Crowley, a great Christian businesswoman and the founder of Home Interiors and Gifts, once said, "We are free to the point of choice, then the choice controls the chooser."

—1987 to 1997—

There is an old song entitled, "What a Difference a Day Makes." Well, in our case, "What a Difference a *Decade* Makes! I wish I could tell you that by applying the dozen Bee's I shared with you in the first edition of *I Can. You Can Too!* my life has been perfect. I wish I could, but life is not perfect.

While there has been so much more good than bad, more positive than negative, more hope than hopelessness, and significantly more encouragement than discouragement, the truth is: Life is Tough!

Dr. Scott Peck began his book, *The Road Less Traveled*, with the phrase, "Life is difficult." That may seem simple and obvious, but it is true! Now before we all throw up our hands and head out for one of the "pity parties" we talked about earlier, let me hurry to say that there is good news. Each experience, good and not-so-good, CAN be a great learning opportunity — if we maintain the proper perspective.

To help keep the proper perspective, I felt it was very important to bring you up to date on my life and family. Someone said, "It's a poor storyteller who is not creative enough to tell a story better than it happened." To keep the facts straight and hopefully to add insight and interest, family and friends have added their thoughts. Their comments are shown in italics on the following pages.

I must tell you that I did not see or read these comments before they were edited into the manuscript. They were inserted by our editorial staff and the great people at Honor Books. And while I am greatly flattered by the comments, I can only say that I hope these folks didn't stretch their credibility too much!

My only input was to ask everyone to be factual and to share joys as well as heartaches, because life is made of sunshine as well as rain, and both are required to make a rainbow.

My prayer is that you have found (and will continue to find) something in these pages that encourages you to say, "I can relate to that. If she can do it, I can too!"

Teacher, Joyce Rowe: *"Reading **I Can. You Can Too!** came at a critical time in my life. I had just experienced the death of my 20-year-old son due to a drunk driver. I was trying to find my way in a muddled world of grief and to make sense out of a senseless tragedy. My heart and my head were at such different levels.*

When I read the book and realized the many traumatic events that Mamie had endured and risen above, it gave me the hope that I was needing. It made me realize I could make it.

So many times in our life God brings an event or person to us just when we think we cannot go on. Mamie McCullough was that person to me. She gave me hope when I felt hopeless, strength when I had none, and the vision of a better day ahead."

 — A DOZEN BEE's FOR SUCCESS —

1. BEE THERE

During one of the most difficult times in my life, Zig Ziglar, his precious wife Jean, and my extended family working with the Zig Ziglar Corporation were incredibly supportive. I will always be grateful to these wonderful people for demonstrating the importance of our first bee: Bee There.

Words fail when I try to express the appreciation and love I felt from so many after Don's death. The years following were difficult at best, but I made the commitment to Bee There for them too.

Eight years later in 1989, about 18 months after *I Can. You Can Too!* was published, I realized that my time at the Zig Ziglar Corporation had come to an end. After much soul-searching and prayer, I made the decision to risk the security of working for this multi-million-dollar corporation by leaving and forming my own business.

Zig was very kind in expressing his desire for me to stay with ZZC. He said, "Now Miss Mamie, your leaving just doesn't seem right to me. I had thought we would always be working together."

"So did I," I explained, "but after evaluating what God would have me do with my life, I am convinced that this is an appropriate time for me to form my own organization. And besides, we will always be working together because we stand for the same principles, teach many of the same concepts, and as Christians, will be spending eternity together in heaven. The only difference is your payroll will be slightly lighter!"

"Is there anything I can do to change your mind?" Zig asked. He obviously wanted to persuade me to stay, but could see the resolve in my eyes and hear the determination in my voice.

"No," I answered quietly but forcefully. I had visualized this scene many times before it actually occurred, and from my perspective there would be no turning back. "Zig, you are a great motivator and a dear friend. I have more respect for you and Jean than you can imagine.

"From a business perspective, I feel that I have done all for you and your company that is possible — and you have done so much for me. I could go through the rest of my career here and be very comfortable; however, as I teach others, we don't *go* through life, we *grow* through life. For me to continue to *grow*, I must *grow* out on my own."

"Then I will help you in any way possible," Zig assured me. "Miss Mamie, if there is anything you need, just let me know." As I expressed my appreciation and left Zig's office, each of us had tears in our eyes. Even though I was leaving, Zig was still supportive. He understands the importance of being there!

— RISK —

My children were in elementary and junior high school. I exchanged a beautifully decorated office with a secretary sitting just outside my door, for a desk and a telephone at the foot of my bed in my home.

As a single parent with the expensive years of college ahead, the decision must have seemed risky from a financial perspective. However, I knew that I could make a good living for my family and just as importantly have more time to spend with the children in their formative years. Since Don's death, I had been forced to Bee There for others — now it was time for me to be there for my children and myself.

Oldest Daughter, Patti: *"Mom has always been there for me. From my earliest memories of sitting in front of the bathroom mirror with her fixing my hair, to my Wedding Day in June of 1996, Mom has always been there for me. My mother prepared me for life. She knows the world will not always be kind, but she let me know that she will always be there for me and always defend me and love me unconditionally."*

✦ 2. BEE YOURSELF

Looking back on being a single parent provides a much better perspective than living through this period. Have I mentioned that life is tough?!

The children and I discussed the advantages and disadvantages of bringing in a "live-in" housekeeper and determined that having a lady to help us was a great idea. Each of the dear, sweet, women I hired was well-intentioned and a good person, but this did not make them appropriate for our family.

One dear soul believed that TV wrestling was real but that man had never walked on the moon. When 7-year-old Brian pointed this out at dinner one evening, I knew we had a problem. And of course there was the sweeper queen who swept so much dirt and dust under the carpeting that our floors looked like the Smokey Mountains (or at least a many-humped camel).

All this occurred despite the fact that I interviewed carefully, checked references, and even had friends do additional interviews. Let me repeat myself and say I am grateful to each and every person we have had in our home to help. Although we may have disagreed on some issues, I do not question their integrity or intentions.

Here is my point: I hope you will hire me to come to your school, church, or company to train your staff and work with your people. I would not recommend you hire me to select a housekeeper for you!

Son, Brian: *"There is more to Mamie McCullough than being an author and speaker. She always goes the extra mile. She has given up so much for my sisters and me to be able to enjoy life to the fullest! She has done all she possibly can to be sure our home was a happy and loving home and that we were all happy!"*

During this time I really had the lesson of Bee Yourself reinforced. At times I "went along to get along" with housekeepers because of a busy schedule, or overindulged the children to "keep the peace." After hiring and firing far too many housekeepers, I even agreed to let the children live with their grandparents during the week and go to school in Brownwood, Texas. This meant I had to make the four-hour drive from Dallas to the farm to be with them on the weekends.

The reasons were excellent: My busy travel schedule, no house-keeper I was completely comfortable with, grandparents who loved the children, great schools, daily supervision by loved ones, less worry on my part about the children. But the idea was unworkable. We needed to live together as a family. One of the reasons I left the Zig Ziglar Corporation was to spend more time with the children, and now I was seeing them only on weekends.

Again after much prayer, I made the decision to Bee Myself. I brought the children home to Dallas to live with me. To an objective observer, this might seem a happy ending to a sad story. However, those of you who have had a child scream, "I hate you," and slam the door understand how even when you are confident that you must bee yourself, you can still question major decisions. My two girls struggled the most with moving back to Dallas, but time is truly the great healer.

Youngest daughter Jennifer: *"As I got older, I realized what a sacrifice my mom made for us. I learned how to not only be a daughter but also a friend to her. My mom is a strong woman and I hope one day to be the courageous and loving woman that she is."*

3. BEE A SELF-STARTER

When I opened my own business I was reminded of the importance of the third bee: Bee A Self-Starter. You may have seen the following quote:

> Every morning in Africa, a gazelle awakens knowing that it must outrun the fastest lion if it wants to stay alive;
>
> Every morning a lion wakes up knowing that it must run faster than the slowest gazelle or it will starve to death;
>
> It makes no difference whether you are a lion or a gazelle; when the sun comes up, you had better start running!

The author is unknown, but the point is right on target! Having the responsibilities that are associated with operating and maintaining a business causes you to get up each morning running! I was fortunate to have several friends who stepped forward to counsel and encourage me as I opened the doors of Mamie McCullough and Associates. One gentleman did such a great job that I married him!

Husband, Herschel Wells: *"Mamie and I attended the same Sunday school class at Prestonwood Baptist Church here in Dallas, Texas. The first time I saw her, I knew she was the most unusual and unique person I had ever laid eyes on! As I "watched from a distance" over several months, it became obvious to me that her class, charm, warmth, intelligence, sincerity and sense of humor were overshadowed only by her godly spirit.*

Watching Mamie deal with Patti, Brian, and Jennifer is a real insight into how to treat people the way they would like to be treated, assure them they are loved, and help them recognize their personal value and worth. As a matter of fact, after Mamie and I dated for a period of time, I came up with what I thought was the perfect plan.

I Can, You Can Too!

Mamie loved those children so much and treated them so well that I decided I wanted to be adopted! Much to my short-term displeasure and long-term happiness, she refused to adopt me but did agree to marry me!"

🐝 4. BEE A RESPONDER

Herschel and I were married in Dallas on January 31, 1993, in the home of our dear friends, evangelist Dr. Jay Strack and his wonderful wife Diane. Keeping McCullough as my name was Herschel's idea. He felt that due to the many years of being in the public eye as Mamie McCullough, changing my name just didn't make sense.

In addition, Herschel was very sensitive to three teenagers having their mother change her name. Herschel is very secure with himself and recognizes my love for him, so the name change was not important to him. I agreed to continue working as Mamie McCullough for business reasons, even though I am very proud to be Mrs. Herschel Wells.

Oldest Daughter, Patti: *"I will be the first to tell you that Herschel and I did not get along when we met. I saw him as someone taking away precious time that I might be spending with my mom. God softens hearts and breaks down walls, and He has done exactly that the last few years. I now see Herschel as a strong protector and warrior for my mom. He is her companion and the person she can bounce ideas off of. He has helped my mother tremendously in her work.*

I have never seen Herschel complain. He does get tired, but he never complains. He is a great businessman, and my husband, Matt, seeks his advice often."

Herschel is my "silent giant" as he goes about handling our

important, behind-the-scenes work in such a quiet and tremendous way. Our clients and friends don't always realize all that is involved in making presentations, leading seminars, writing books, and developing training materials.

The myriad of details is mind-boggling. Our business is similar to the duck on the pond: On top of the water there is the appearance of a smooth, efficient, and effective gliding movement; under the water, the duck is paddling like mad! Without Herschel, I would be hard-pressed to stay afloat.

Son, Brian: "*Herschel is a great guy! I love him dearly! I think he has a lot of qualities my dad had. The thing I love the most about Hersh is that he is very supportive and he loves my mother and won't let anything bad happen to her. It means a lot to me to see my mother happy. Basically, he is just an all-around cool guy who would do anything for any of us!*"

— THE V.P. —

Herschel often laughlingly calls himself the Vice President of Lifting and Loading. He drives to almost every engagement to make my books, tapes, and educational and instructional programs available to participants. Program participants can use these "follow-up" materials to review and determine how to apply the information in their lives.

Any time your hands are busy but your mind is not (traveling, cooking, sewing, working in the yard) you can be putting the good, clean, pure, powerful, and positive information of your choosing into your mind by listening to audio cassette tapes. Just before going to sleep at night is an excellent time to read a few pages of a book, magazine, or article so that your subconscious mind can review the information while you sleep.

If you are not programming your mind, then someone else is, and they may not have your best interests at heart. Without Herschel's help, it would be nearly impossible to get this information into people's hands.

Youngest Daughter, Jennifer: "*Herschel has been a strong support that my mom has needed for a long time. When he first came into our lives, his presence was not so welcome — but Herschel kept showing us he loved us and that he loved our mom very much. He stepped into our family and accepted three children that weren't even his.*

He has never pushed himself on us or tried to fill the position of my father. Through time he has allowed us to love him for who he is. Herschel is a strong, intelligent man who would do anything for me and my family. He has been there for me when I needed him most, and he treats me like I am his own daughter."

— MISSION ACCOMPLISHED? —

Herschel is one of those unique people who has accomplished what he set out to accomplish in life. He was an athlete in high school and college, graduated from the University of Texas, was a Distinguished Flying School Graduate (and finished second in his class) of the United States Air Force, and for six years flew jet planes while serving as a jet pilot instructor.

After leaving the Air Force, Herschel worked in the fast-paced and exciting world of financial trading. This is probably the only industry that moves faster than the jets he was flying! I wondered why everyone got so quiet when Herschel spoke until I found out he worked for E. F. Hutton (you show your age and TV viewing habits if you "get" that one). He also spent 10 years on the

Chicago Board of Trade. As incredibly intelligent and wonderfully wise as he is, I love Herschel simply because he is Herschel.

Herschel: "*I have been fortunate in doing most of what I wanted to do in my life. I loved participating in athletics, enjoyed flying jets, and found trading in the financial market to be very exciting! However, as I evaluated my life, I realized that for me, these didn't have the "socially redeeming value" that I had always admired in the "helping" professions (medicine, education, religious service). The greatest joy in my life is working in the background and watching as Mamie gives others the precious gifts of encouragement and hope.*"

In the first edition of *I Can. You Can Too!* I talked about joining the Zig Ziglar Corporation with Don McCullough and my joy in being able to work with him in a career we both saw as a mission. My vision of changing the classrooms I taught in had become a reality; my dream of affecting an entire school came to pass during my time as a principal; Don and I felt we were on the threshold of reaching people on a larger scale when he suddenly and tragically passed away.

Despite the tragedies of life, I know and understand that God is so good! Today, He has allowed me the opportunity of reviving the dream of making a difference with someone I love and trust in Herschel. Herschel has taught me to Bee A Responder and learn to deal with life's difficulties in a positive manner. In the process, he has also helped develop my vision as we learn together to Bee A Goal Setter. Our goal is very simple. We want to change the world — one person at a time.

5. BEE A GOAL-SETTER

In 1983, a prominent business executive with a major soft-drink company resigned his post to become the president of a fledgling computer company, an unproven organization that offered no guarantees. Why? The excitement of one man's vision and the question he was asked: "Do you want to spend the rest of your life selling sugared water, or do you want a chance to change the world?"

The executive was Pepsico's John Sculley, the visionary was Apple Computer co-founder Steven Jobs. For more than 10 years these men had a great impact on the world through their world of computers. Today they face new challenges. Apple Computers is faced with some major decisions in the later part of the 1990's that will determine how or even *if* they enter the next century. If these two men maintain their vision, I certainly wouldn't bet against Sculley and Jobs!

Here is my point: "Without a vision, the people will perish" (Proverbs 29:18). If you and I are going to learn to Bee A Goal-Setter, we must have a vision. Without somewhere to go, how will we know which road to take to get there?

Some will snicker when I say our goal is to change the world, even when I add "one person at a time." But I will not react negatively to the nay-sayers of this world. I will respond positively and continue: Hoping, praying and believing that others will learn the lesson the jogger learned in the following story.

— AN EXERCISE IN FUTILITY —

A jogger made his way along the beach in the early morning hours after a storm littered the sand with debris. Among the limbs and shells were what looked like hundreds if not thousands of starfish that had been washed ashore and were dying.

As he ran, the jogger noticed something or some-one off in the distance. As he got closer, he saw what turned out to be an elderly gentleman stoop-ing down to pick up one starfish after the other, and throwing each of them back into the ocean to live another day.

The jogger, recognizing the elderly gentleman's exercise in futility, asked why he would waste his time with a few when saving all the starfish seemed impossible. "Sir," the jogger asked, "What could it possibly matter?"

With the wisdom accumulated in years of experi-ence in living and loving life, the elderly man reached down and tossed another starfish into the ocean and said, "It only matters to this one!"

I have been blessed in so many ways that it would take a book larg-er than *Webster's Dictionary* to even begin telling you about each one. However, my greatest blessing was receiving my M.A.M.A. Degree. My belief and my prayer is that my greatest achievement in life, and my greatest contribution to society, will be the three children with whom God has blessed me.

Patricia Lynn McCullough was born on March 9, 1973; Brian Wilson McCullough on April 8, 1975; and Jennifer Ann McCullough on September 12, 1976. As you mathematicians can see, I no longer have teenagers. We made it through the Difficult D's: Dating and Driving. And, we all survived!

I have only two goals for my children: First, that they would serve the Lord; and second, that they would receive good training so they could one day have good jobs that would allow them to pay my social security!

I have also promised my children two things: One degree and one wedding — in that order!

🐝 6. BEE A GOOD-FINDER

Son, Brian: *"My mom is the definition of what a MOM should be — and, she is the kind of woman I would like to marry. She is loving, supportive, funny, very smart, and very strong. My favorite impression is the way I feel walking in my front door. She is standing there and waiting for a hug and kiss from her boy! Her sincere love and joy in loving me is the thing I value the most."*

Our oldest, Patti, is a graduate of Texas A&M University. She received her degree in Speech Communications. In June of 1996 she married another A&M graduate, Matthew Wyman, an engineer. Matt is an answer to prayer, because he is not only a wonderful helpmate to Patti, but is the spiritual leader in their home. He is such a fine, intelligent, and strong young man! We are so very happy to have Matt as a part of our family.

The wedding was held at Prestonwood Baptist Church on June 1, 1996, in Dallas, Texas. Youngest daughter Jennifer was Patti's maid of honor, and Brian stood in for his dad and gave away the bride. More than a few tears of joy were shed on this magnificent day!

The wedding reception was held at Southfork Ranch (neither J. R. nor Bobby were there — once again, your age and TV habits will help you) and many of my family made the trip from Georgia and other places near and far to be a part of this most precious event.

One of my dear friends and prayer partners, Diane Strack, said,

"Mamie, it's a good thing your dress doesn't have buttons, because if it did they would be popping off!" Yes, I will admit to being very proud of my little girl in the process of becoming such a wonderful woman.

Oldest Daughter Patti: "*Giving and more giving is the only way I can describe what my mother did for Matt and me for our wedding. The night before the wedding, Mom and I sat in the middle of our den unwrapping presents and reflecting. The next morning, my sister Jennifer and I woke up to a fabulous breakfast.*

The dining room table was set with our finest china and beautiful fresh flowers. The food was incredible: warm grits, eggs, bacon, homemade biscuits and all the trimmings! We had such a sweet time of fellowship. Mother always adds the perfect touch. She is one of a kind and I am so grateful she is mine.

No one will ever love me the way she does, no one will ever sacrifice like she has, and no one will ever take her place. She is my mother, and she deserves a standing ovation for how she has raised her children! I am who I am today only because of my mother. She has instilled in me the love of Christ, the strong morals, and my outlook on life.

I pray daily that my husband, and the children we will one day have, will see the woman my mother is in me. When they do, I will have succeeded in life. My mother's crown in heaven will be one filled with jewels like no other, and her mansion beautiful. God looks down on her and is pleased."

7. BEE POSITIVE

Our middle child, son Brian, attended Howard Payne University in Brownwood, Texas. I graduated from HPU in 1963, and unless you have a child who has attended the same school which you attended, you cannot imagine the thrill.

Brian was diagnosed with Attention Deficit Disorder as a sophomore in college. I sometimes tease him and say I diagnosed him ADD-D, which stands for ADD — Deliberate! But truthfully, I am very proud of the way Brian has dealt with his challenge.

When the diagnosis was made, we set about finding out all we could about ADD. This led Brian to be on medication to help control the symptoms and focus his attention. After about six months, Brian made the decision that he did not want to be dependent on medication for the rest of his life, so with information, inspiration, and education he learned to compensate and functions extremely well today without medication.

ADD and ADHD are very serious problems facing parents in our society today. The great news is that ADD need not be a limiting factor on a child leading a happy and productive childhood. Once again, the difference is perspective.

If ADD is used as an excuse for continued aberrant behavior, then the diagnosis was wasted. If it is used as a "point of departure" for seeking solutions and helping a child function in life by taking personal responsibility for his or her behavior, the diagnosis has been worthwhile.

Brian determined he wanted to leave college after his junior year to enter the business world. Leaving college also means he has chosen to pay his own way. He enjoys having his own apartment, and we love having him in the home in which he grew up (my home will always be his home). I will always be waiting at the door "with a hug and a kiss for my boy," no matter how old "my boy" becomes!

Brian: *"Most people know that I am a caring and loving person who doesn't stress about most things. I would give my friends whatever I had if they needed it. Basically I live one day at a time — and I give 110 percent of my ability!"*

Brian is doing well in his current career. He writes "thank-you" notes to customers, walks them to their cars, remembers names, greets customers personally when they return to the shop, and consistently displays a very positive attitude. Brian has a vision for the future that will allow him to be successful at whatever he does in life!

8. BEE A GOOD INFLUENCE

Jennifer is my teacher-child. I have known she was going to be a teacher since she was in the first grade. Shortly after she started school, I found her in her room one Saturday morning with her dolls all lined up around her and she was teaching them! As I walked in the room I overheard her say to her favorite doll Kellie, "I've just about had it up to here with you!" Wonder where she heard that?

Even in high school Jennifer spent her afternoons working with the special education kids, and throughout her schooling she has continued to be involved with children. She will soon get her degree from Howard Payne University in Elementary Special Education. She has a heart for the at-risk kids and has been working part-time after school teaching kids to read.

Jennifer: *"The trials in my life have made me a stronger person. I always try to remember that God has his arms around me and is molding me into a woman who can use the trials in my life to help others. I still deal with the pain in some areas, but I know that I will make it through hard times, because I have my eyes focused on the goal.*

I truly feel that God has chosen some people to "run a marathon" in life. I feel that I am one of those people. He is preparing me for that journey everyday, and I am training to finish this race. I know that He has great things planned for those who follow Him.

My mom has been an important influence in my life. I have realized how to deal with the trials of life by watching her strength. Mom is a busy woman who tries to help others because of the pain she has felt in her own life. Although she is so very busy, she still finds time for the most important things: Her relationship with God, her family, and her loved ones.

In our lives we have gone through so many of the same things. I truly believe that we went through those things so that we would be able to help each other. We have become so close through all of the hard times that our family has gone through, and I thank God for our close relationship."

9. BEE PROFESSIONAL

When I think of professionalism, one of the first people to come to mind is my friend Dr. Grace Pilot. Meticulously organized, Grace is a person who grabs onto projects with great tenacity — and always follows through. As a matter of fact, she is one of the few people I know who is a textbook example of all our BEES! In addition, Grace is so humble that I had to prevail on our friendship just to get her to let me tell you about the role she has played in my life!

Grace is one of ten children, and despite humble beginnings has accomplished a great deal in her life (and she isn't done yet!). Nobody is around Grace for more than five minutes before finding out she is completely committed to her church, her family, and her ten grandchildren. She is generous, kind, considerate, and thoughtful. It is impossible to out-give Grace Pilot! To our children she is "Aunt Grace." We call her Amazing Grace because she truly is!

Grace Pilot: *"I often think of the section of **I Can. You Can Too!** where Mamie describes her initial meeting with Dr. Guy Newman. In the book we read, "Dr. Newman told me many years later that he took one look at me and thought to himself, 'There stands the scrawniest, the homeliest, and the saddest child with the least amount of potential I have ever seen in my entire life...and I have got to encourage her to stay!'"*

I can't help but think that even in his wildest dreams, as positive as Dr. Newman was, would he believe that the child standing in front of him would graduate from Howard Payne; be a manager and executive in the construction industry, direct sales, as well as training and consulting; become a high school administrator; write books that would be read by hundreds of thousands of people; develop school curriculum, and eventually serve as a Trustee on the Howard Payne Board of Directors?

As much of a visionary as Dr. Newman was, I wonder if he could ever have envisioned the Mamie D. McCullough Athletic Complex, which was built and named in Mamie's honor in 1994."

Like her name, Grace is most gracious! She would be the last person to say so, but Grace Pilot was the driving force financially and inspirationally behind the creation of the "Mamie D. McCullough Athletic Complex." In the foyer of this beautiful and modern building is a portrait of Grace and myself, with a plaque that says, "The House That Friendship Built."

Grace is absolutely correct when she says I was honored to have a building on my college campus named after me...and I didn't even have to die! Words could not express the honor I feel. If you have ever felt undeserving, you will know exactly how I felt when the idea was proposed.

Look again at the picture of the house in which I was born and ask yourself if this looks like the home of someone whom a college building will be named after. Remember, it's not where you start, it's where you finish that counts. I have worked on my "deserve level" and I am thrilled, honored, and humbled by the kindness of all those involved!

Teacher, Joyce Rowe: "*Mamie and I attended Howard Payne at the same time. I worked part-time for Dr. Newman and knew that Mamie was living with the Newmans. In my eyes she was the rich girl from Georgia who dressed like a model, was always too busy to speak, and was too good to live in the dorm. As the years passed, family members would remark that they had heard her speak and asked if I knew her. I would say, "Yes," and go on about my business.*

About five years ago my mother attended a book review where **I Can. You Can Too!** *was reviewed. She sent the book to me and insisted I read it. I could not put it down! So many misconceptions in my thinking were brought to light. I realized that the reason Mamie lived with the Newmans was because she was too poor to live in the dorm. I found out she didn't speak because she was so very shy she would break out in a rash. And she dressed so well because she was wearing the college president's wife's clothes!*

This has taught me how very wrong we can be about the way we look at people. We must look beneath the surface to the "real" person and not judge by outward appearances. I am so thankful I know the "real" Mamie."

🐝 10. BEE PREPARED

How do you prepare to give people the right information at the right time? The only way I know to deal with life's responsibilities is by doing the best you can with what you have on a daily basis — and that, to me, is success!

I have not been directly involved with promoting, marketing, and selling the "I CAN" course since 1993. I have always been active in promoting, marketing, and encouraging others in the "I CAN" Way of Life.

Without direct involvement in the course and curriculum, I have been able to devote my energies to the areas where I can have the most positive impact: educators, church groups, and businesses. As a matter of fact, my presentations have moved from 60 percent schools and 40 percent businesses to 40 percent schools, 40 percent churches, and 20 percent businesses — the right distribution for me!

Teacher, Bruce Layne: "*I Can. You Can Too! touches every aspect of life. This book helps in becoming a better parent, which makes you a better teacher, and becoming a better teacher makes you a better parent! You become a better teacher and parent by becoming a better listener. I learned from listening to Mamie and reading her book that the best teachers teach with their heart, not their head. Thank you, Mamie. Reading your story is all we really need to turn up our hopeometer!*"

Efficiency is doing things right and *Effectiveness* is doing the right things. Since my focus has changed, I have written two additional books: *Get It Together and Remember Where You Put It*, and

I Can. You Can Too!

Mama's Rules for Livin'.

Currently, I am finalizing my next book, *I Wish I Had Someone To Take Up For Me: Help For Those Who Need Hope and Healing*. This book looks at the many different types of abuse so prevalent in our society, contains some of the details of my own experiences, looks at ways to prevent abuse, and discusses how to get on with the abundant life we have all been promised.

My speaking opportunities have grown, both in quantity and quality, and the seminars have been very well received. I conduct seminars on many different topics, and these sessions run from one to three days. The one I do most frequently is Y.E.S. (You Encourage Success) seminar for educators.

In just three days I discuss creating a positive school climate, accepting multi-cultural diversity, demonstrating professionalism as an educator, managing stress, building communication skills, preventing drug abuse, and learning how to deal with difficult students, parents, and administrators!

Linda Macy, Ed.S., Elementary Principal, and Ted O. Spessard, Ed.D, Superintendent of Schools: "*Miss Mamie's philosophy is fundamental to the good life. It is also our philosophy. It works in our lives and we share it with all our staff and students. Miss Mamie has been to our school, shared her message, and we carried it on. This approach makes coming to school every day a joy for children and adults.*"

In addition to a number of projects, I have also taken the time to work on my personal dreams. Isn't it amazing how the "tyranny of the urgent" will keep us from dreaming? For many years I have been praying about a special dream that I want to share with you.

I call my dream, "House of Hope."

House of Hope is a retreat center situated on a small lake with large shade trees scattered over rolling hills. Each room in the House of Hope is a "theme" room (western, Victorian, country, etc.) with its own private bath. There is a giant playroom with game tables, a juke box, an old-fashioned phone booth, an antique barber's chair, church pews, Brumbey Rockers, and lounge chairs galore! The huge porch goes around three sides of the two-story home.

The House of Hope is dedicated to providing a safe haven for those who need to retreat from life's daily battles. At House of Hope, the visitor will receive rest, inspiration, education, and direction on how to give himself or herself permission to release guilt and hopeless feelings.

Each person will have the opportunity to learn that they did not cause the majority of these needless feelings and thoughts. The House of Hope provides an atmosphere that will allow people to understand that many, if not most, of the bad things that happened were not their fault.

By now I hope you are wondering exactly where the House of Hope is located. Well, so am I. Today it exists only in my imagination. But tomorrow...!

I beelieve the research, organization, freedom to dream, and intensive focus taken to plan, accomplish, and visualize these projects have helped me prepare to do the work God would have me do.

— THE PRICE OF EXCELLENCE —

Settling for mediocrity, doing just enough to get by, or having a job as opposed to the job having you, are all symptoms of the deep attitudinal problem that pervades our society. These problems are not restricted to the field of education. This attitude is prevalent in all walks of life: schools, offices, and even churches.

In general, people will not or have a hard time accepting youth, new ideas, or change. In our multi-cultural society, if we do not learn to observe without criticism, understand that "different" does not always mean wrong, and accept others' differences "until we can walk a mile in their shoes," we are not going to have all the good things God wants us to have!

Several years ago I met a first-grade teacher, Lynne Wyatt. She and my Patti had become good friends through the youth activities at our church. Lynne became one of our family from the first time she came to our home for Sunday dinner.

Lynne is the type of person we all hope will teach our children. She does extra work during the summer and on weekends, as well as spending many school nights doing the "little things that make the big difference": bulletin boards, motivational quotes (Heartitudes), special events calendars, posters, inspirational pictures, seasonal classroom decorations, and many other innovative ideas that create a great learning environment for her students.

Lynne's first teaching assignment was in a troubled area of Dallas. She loved the children, but got little or no support from the children's families. She persevered, and after finishing a very diffi- cult year, moved to another school.

Lynne's first year at her new school was wonderful! The parents were involved with their children and the school was blessed with a principal who was an outstanding professional educator and leader. Lynne seemed to be flourishing in this positive environment.

Near the end of her second year in teaching, Lynne came by our home to visit. Imagine my surprise to find she was unhappy and depressed. The sadness in her eyes gave her away, and she was much more quiet and reserved than I had ever noticed.

Lynne said, "Mrs. McCullough, I'm not going to teach next year, and I was wondering if you could help me become a flight attendant?" She knew I was a Frequent Flyer in the American Airlines Advantage Gold Club, and thought this might help.

"Lynne," I replied, "you know I will help you in any way I can. The airlines will surely hire you because you are a top-notch person in every way! If you think it would make a difference, I will write a letter of recommendation for you."

"Good, because I not only need your help with a letter of recommendation, but I need you to advise me on who to talk to, what to say, and how to lose five pounds!"

Patti and I sat down with her and discussed how she could set goals, gather information, and make good choices in each of her areas of concern. After discussing everything we could think of on how to pursue an opportunity for employment with the airlines, I finally asked, "Lynne, what happened? I was under the impression your new school was as good as your first school was bad! What changed?"

"Nobody likes me!" she blurted out.

"Nobody?" I asked, using an old sales technique that is helpful in discovering people's objections. If the sales person will repeat the prospect's statement in the form of a question and then remain quiet, true objections will be revealed.

"Well..." she stammered, obviously having trouble determining exactly who didn't like her.

I Can. You Can Too!

"You mean the principal doesn't like you?" I asked.

"Oh, no," she said quickly, "I work with a great principal who really respects my work. He said so on all my evaluations!"

"Well then, I guess it is the parents who don't like you." I prodded. "Oh, no!" she exclaimed, "They sent me notes, cards, and even gifts. I have never heard of a group of parents being so kind to a teacher as my students' parents were to me."

"Obviously, we have found the culprits," I teased. "It must be those rug-rats, the crumb-crunchers, the urchins, those rotten children you try to teach!" A look of shock crossed her face until she saw my smile and realized I was being facetious.

She relaxed a little and chuckled, "Oh Miss Mamie, you know I love those kids and they love me too!"

We let the silence sit for a moment. I knew who didn't like her, and she was beginning to see the light as well. Finally, Lynne broke the silence. "Some days they won't even talk to me," she said sadly.

"Yes, I understand," I continued, "And let me guess the rest. They don't include you in activities outside school, they get really quiet when you come into the teachers' lounge, they make fun of your working so hard, and they even give the children you teach a hard time."

Lynne's eyes grew wide with astonishment! "How did you know?"

"I haven't been in the classroom for many years now," I explained, "but teachers haven't changed much since the time I had the same experience you are having."

You see, regardless of profession, there are always going to be some in your field who will be jealous of those who want to excel. There was a part of the faculty who chose to "freeze" Lynne out of their lives because they couldn't or wouldn't be a part of hers: her commitment to excellence, to doing whatever it takes to get the job done, to the future of our country, and even our world.

Fortunately, the majority of professional educators *are* committed to excellence. The phrase is worth repeating: Those who affect the life of a child will affect generations to come.

Lynne was offered a flight attendant's job with a major airline. She came by to see me the day she had to make the decision to return the contract to the school or commit to the airline. "You just have to help me make this decision," she pleaded.

Thinking back to the story I shared with you a few pages ago about John Sculley and Steven Jobs, I asked her a simple question. "Would you prefer to serve coffee the rest of your life or would you rather make a difference in our society, our country, and possibly our world?"

How often in life do we recover from an initial disappointment to find that "it" (the heartache, the frustration, the pain, the disappointment, the misunderstanding) is in our own best interest? Though we cannot see the truth at the time, we later learn that, as Romans 8:28 says, "All things work together for good for those that know and love the Lord."

All things are not good in and of themselves, but all can work together for good! So often our faith is rewarded more than we could ever hope for — the challenge is timing. Our rewards don't always occur as quickly as we would wish!

Lynne discovered that all the trouble she had had, and even trying to enter a different profession, were designed to show her exactly where she belonged, what her purpose in life was. She also learned the price of excellence, and that it is well worth paying. I am very pleased to report to you that Lynne Wyatt is making a difference in the world! She is now teaching at a school for accelerated students and doing a beautiful job!

Please don't misunderstand. Flight attendants perform a most important function in the very vital industry of travel and transportation! My point here, however, is that Lynne was not *called* to be a flight attendant. Where serving passengers on an airline is a most important calling — especially to those of us who fly frequently! — this was not Lynne's gift.

Becoming an educator is definitely a specialized calling. What other profession employs so many people with so much education making so little money? Professional educators teach because it is a mission, a passion, and a high calling.

Once again, "Those who affect the life of a child will affect generations to come." Lynne Wyatt learned to pursue her passion and consequently she is a great teacher — one of the best!

11. BEE CONSISTENT

In speaking to educators for over twenty years, I often begin my speeches by saying, "We do not have an 'education problem,' we have a 'society problem.'" And what I mean is this: As parents, we need to take responsibility for our children.

The book of Proverbs states, "Train up a child in the way he should go and he will not depart from it." Many children grow up angry, rebellious, and unhappy because they have never had anyone to love and train them. Dr. James Dobson's book, *Parenting Isn't for Cowards*, is a great resource if you want more information in this incredibly important area.

Principal, Melinda Swanson: *"Mamie, you have made me laugh and made me cry. As I look back, this book has had one of the most lasting impressions on my life. I pick it up when I've had a bad day and it feeds my soul. I pick it up when I've had a good day and it reinforces that 'I CAN!'"*

As I said earlier, my mother brought us up with four basic rules: Love others. Work hard. Go to church. Stay clean. Oh that we as parents could teach these basic rules! You see, children naturally crave structure. When parents have the courage to provide guidelines, everyone benefits.

One of the biggest challenges we face heading into the 21st century is the challenge of consistency — especially in establishing boundaries. "Situational" ethics often mean, "Whatever feels good at the moment is okay." Taking the "path of least resistance" has become our national pastime.

Parents, teachers, business men and women, church staff members, churchgoers, and almost everyone in our population is longing to understand what is good or bad, right or wrong, appropriate or inappropriate. We all need a sense of the line of demarcation — that point which we must not cross. And we need to have the line pointed out consistently.

The next time you pass a school yard, look to see if there is a fence around the playground area. If there is, you will notice that children will use the entire area — all the resources that are available. They will run right up to the fence and everywhere in between.

I Can. You Can Too!

If there is no fence, you will notice that the children will group in the center of the playground. Occasionally an "adventurous soul" will wander away, but the *majority* of the children use the *minority* of the space (resources) available. When we maintain consistent boundaries, we encourage use of all the resources available.

The first time my Patti was home from college, she was having a great time visiting high school friends. At about 11:15 p.m., she announced that she was going two doors down the street to play bridge with some of her buddies. I had known these young adults since they were in junior high. They had been in and out of our home (and us theirs) for years, so there was no danger in Patti going.

I simply stated, "You aren't going to have much time to play and still get home by 12." Patti rolled her eyes as only our own children can do (I tried to demonstrate her eye rolling at one of my speeches, but my contacts popped out, so I don't do that anymore), and said, "But Mother, I'm in college now!"

I said, "Yes, Patti, since I send a check to Texas A&M on a regular basis, I am well aware you are in college now. However, in this home, we always operate under the Golden Rule, so you will need to be in by midnight."

"What in the world does being in by midnight have to do with the Golden Rule?"

Pausing for emphasis I answered, "Patti, it is very simple. The one who has the gold, rules. Right now you are on my payroll — and I am glad that you are! I have enjoyed clothing, feeding, sheltering, educating, and loving you into adulthood. When you go off the payroll, you will make your own policies, rules, and guidelines. Until then, you will be in by 12." And she was!

Patti: *"People always ask if we go through real life problems. YES! We are a normal family and go through trials. My family is so important to me, and we enjoy (and work through) life together. My mom is God's Proverbs 31 woman.*

She is strong, but weak; giving above and beyond at all times; loving her family unconditionally, and working hard to provide for us. She makes sure her children want for nothing. She is soft but can stand firm. She is an incredible businesswoman, and yet she has a heart to reach thousands. She is my mother — God gave her to me and she is one of the biggest blessings of my life."

Allowing Patti to do what she wanted to do would have been much easier than standing firm; however, "permissiveness is neglect of duty." As parents, managers, teachers, and just plain *human beings,* we must all say what we mean and have the courage to stand by our convictions!

Standing by our convictions allows us to establish familiar boundaries which in turn allows us to use all the resources available to us. Having the courage to do what is right, but not necessarily easy, demonstrates true love. Decisions made consistently with love and prayer lead to closer relationships.

12. BEE LOVING AND CARING

I grew up in a home that was the model of loving and caring, so I would like to take the opportunity to introduce you to my family. The man I mentioned in Chapter 5 called them "the hicks from the sticks," which said much more about him than it did them! Here is my wonderful family of whom I am so proud.

Mallory Darlington was my Daddy. Unfortunately, I have very few memories of him. I wish I could have known him. My mother and sisters tell me he was warm, kind, caring, and a hard worker. I know he loved my mother very much, as she did him.

Bertha Darlington was my mother. For a lady who could neither read nor write, she graduated Magna Cum Laude from the School of Life's Experiences. She took an impossible situation, raising 9 children under the most difficult of circumstances, and gave us a happy home with a loving mother and loving brothers and sisters.

Daughter Patti: "*Some of the sweetest time I spent with my mother was when she and I would visit my Granny. I will never forget the tree covered road leading into Dixie, and the smell of sweet peach tarts that Granny made for us.*"

Richard Darlington was my oldest brother. Oh, how I wish you could have met my big brother! Had you had the opportunity, you would be very happy to say you had known him. He was witty, fun-loving, and a teaser! He always took time to talk with others, and he always made them feel better for having been in his presence. Richard treated the janitor and the bank president in exactly the same way. He treated every individual with the respect he or she deserved. The world lost a great man in 1965 when Richard Darlington died.

My oldest sister, Voncille Darlington (Taylor), was 16 years old when our Daddy died. Because Richard developed rheumatic fever during this same period, Vonnie had to take on additional responsibilities and help our mother to mother us. I shall always remember Vonnie coming in from work "dead tired" and being greeted with adoration by her younger brothers and sisters. We would treat her like the queen she was by rubbing feet, shoulders, arms, and head. Voncille is the consummate wife, mother, and housekeeper. The rumor in Dixie, Georgia, is that when Vonnie's husband gets up during the night for a snack, she often has the bed made before he can get back!

My sister, Evelyn Darlington (Harmon), was born after Voncille. If you look up "perseverance" (and probably "courage") in the dictionary, you will find a picture of Evelyn as a part of the definition. Evelyn raised 5 children amidst some of life's greatest challenges, and then in her 40's went back to school to become a licensed practical nurse. She received her degree and today works as an LPN in Beaumont, Texas. If I ever think about giving up, I think about Evelyn and know if she can endure what she has endured, then I can too!

June Darlington (Lewis) is my "fragile" sister. She has spent her life battling heart problems and other health concerns, and despite this worked extremely hard for family and friends. Even the horrible migraine headaches she suffered couldn't dampen her sweet and loving spirit. In Clyattville, Georgia, she is known as "Momma June," the lady with the heart of gold. June couldn't weigh over 110 pounds, and I guarantee you that 100 pounds of that is heart!

Mary Lou Darlington (Parker) is my sister who is known world-wide for making the very best 16-layer chocolate cake that ever found its way into any mouth! She bears a striking physical resemblance to our mama and even walks as Mama did. Mary Lou loves being a mom and a friend — and she is incredibly good at both! When it comes to a willingness to work hard and do "whatever it takes," Mary Lou will get the job done! She is not only willing to do the work, but she does it with the greatest of attitudes. You will search long and far before you find a person with Mary Lou's work habits and excellent attitude. She is a rare person!

Douglas Darlington is the quiet brother who goes about helping others with very little fanfare. In a reserved and modest manner, Douglas will cut grass for the widows, run errands for the home-bound, plant and harvest gardens, and do just about anything for those who are unable to help themselves. Since his retirement from the Nabisco Corporation, Douglas goes early or late, does the chores, and returns home before anyone realizes he has gone anywhere. Even the people he serves don't always know it was Douglas who was their guardian angel for the day.

Martha Ann Darlington (Blundell) is the sister closest to my age. As you might remember, Martha was the one I was so jealous of for all those years — and for good reason! She is incredibly beautiful on the inside and the outside, and I love her dearly! She is a great teacher, the role-model of what a pastor's wife should be, and the quintessential servant of others. Martha will cook 20 meals a week for people in their congregation and spend as many hours delivering them as she did preparing them.

Mamie Clare Darlington (McCullough) is the next girl. I hope you are getting to know me better throughout this book!

Joe Darlington was my baby brother. Joe spent the majority of his life in the service and traveled all over the world. Consequently, we didn't get to spend most of Joe's adult life with him. In 1993, Joe retired to Dixie. What a great three years we spent getting to know each other again and catching up on each other's lives. Joe was diagnosed with cancer in March of 1996, and passed away in July.

As you would guess, with 9 brothers and sisters, there were 9 perspectives of what happened during our time in the Darlington home. My prayer is that each of these great people will realize how much I love them, how much I learned from them, how much I respect them, and how proud I am to be a member of the Darlington family.

Then there is my "adopted" sister, Elizabeth Jones-Simpson, who is the epitome of southern class, style and charm. Proverbs 18:24 says, "One who has friends must also be friendly, but there is a friend who sticks closer than a sister." (NKJMS-New King James Mamie Style). Elizabeth is one who is closer than a sister. I also adopted her parents, Carl Winter Jones and Harriet Jones. These beautiful people, who are both 80, celebrated their 60th Wedding Anniversary in January of 1997.

Childhood friend Elizabeth Jones: "*Mamie is without question one of the sweetest-natured people I have ever known. I do truly love her! As a child, she was very shy and not nearly as outgoing as she is today. I often had the feeling there was something she wanted to tell me, but just couldn't. What a tragedy to learn about the abuse all those years later; and what an inspiration to see how Mamie has taken the terrible things that happened and used them to inspire others!*

Mamie talks about how "rich" we were, and how we lived up on the "hard road," but I loved to go to her house. The home was two stories and we loved playing on those steps and running back and forth between floors. There always seemed to be laughter and fun at the Darlington home. We even got to run outside to the well whenever we wanted a drink of water, which I thought was a treat!

As Mamie says, so much of life is in our perspective. I am grateful to God for a friend like Mamie who has helped me keep a better perspective just because she is Mamie!

The proof, as the cliché says, is in the pudding. Mamie almost didn't use the following poem and letter in this bonus chapter because she didn't want people to think she was bragging on herself. I strongly suggested (when you have been friends for over 50 years you can "strongly suggest") that she close this bonus chapter with a poem and letter from daughter Jennifer. I think you will see and hear more about Mamie McCullough in this letter than you have read up to this point."

Following is the letter to which Elizabeth was referring. The story Jennifer refers to in the first sentence of her letter is called *The Giving Tree* by Shel Silverstein, and is published by HarperCollins.

Mom,

"I read this story to my kids in class and I began to cry.* I couldn't help but think about all of the wonderful things that you have done for me this past year and throughout my lifetime. You are truly an unbelievable woman, mother, and friend. I don't know how I could ever thank you enough for all of the little things that you do on a regular basis.

When I was small, we played together and we shared cups of coffee-milk every Sunday morning. As I grew older, we went to girl-scout meetings and took trips to see all of our wonderful but wacky family in Georgia. And as I grew even older, we spent many an afternoon shopping, drinking coffee, and getting our nails and hair done. Now, I am even older. I often times wish I wasn't because I deeply miss the precious time we spent together. Now that I am a big girl, I have begun to realize how difficult it is to balance everything that is most important to you as well as dealing with the world and all of its complications. I realize what you must have gone through raising the three of us by yourself. But the real blessing is that you were not by yourself. You had a loving God who helped you raise three, mother-loving, God-fearing children that you now have to enjoy. I truly am so thankful to you for giving to me even when you had nothing left to give, for allowing time out of your busy schedule to listen to my boy problems, and for instilling the values and morals in me that I will one day pass on to my own children. I hope that I was able to slightly explain how much you mean to me in these few pages. I could go on forever. Your value is more than Rubies. I love you with all of my heart and a little more."

Love always in all ways,

Jennifer

10-02-96

*Shel Silverstein, The Giving Tree (New York: Harper & Row, 1964).

Bee Convicted of Caring and Encouraging in the First Degree

While working on writing *I Can. You Can Too!* I was convinced that the information I was sharing with you could make a difference. Had I been on trial for my life, I could not have been more open or honest in my efforts to say to you, "If I CAN, then You Can Too!"

To be convicted of murder in the first degree, the law requires at least three things. The first is proof there was a murder — which usually means finding a body. Secondly, there must be proof that the accused actually did the deed — which usually involves an eye-witness, and hopefully more than one. In the third place, there must be proof of intent.

To be convicted of Caring and Encouraging in the first degree, the law would require at least three things. The first is proof that someone does actually care about others and encourage them — which usually means finding a well-adjusted, joyful person who is cared for and has been encouraged. Secondly, there must be proof that the accused actually did the deed — which usually involves an eyewitness, and hopefully more than one. In the third place, there must be proof of intent.

Please allow me to submit the following evidence. In the first place, there are people who live hopeless lives. These are people who are stuck in a rut. And as you may know, a rut is nothing in the world but a grave with the ends kicked out!

These "walking zombies" began life with hopes, dreams, plans, and the desire to make a difference in the lives of others. After living for years with little or no care or encouragement, they have to make a conscious effort to be able to put one foot in front of the other to exist. The attitude, "will," or spirit of these people is being or has already been murdered.

However, as you observe life, you will also notice those who have an extra "spring" in their step. These are women and men who seize the day and enjoy each moment of their life as if it will be the last one, because they understand that someday the last moment will actually come.

Someone is definitely helping people move from group one into group two.

Based on your letters, and the kind words you share when we meet in person, my books, tapes, and presentations are encouraging you and those you care about to seek the more abundant life (which is available to all of us). Many of you are actual eyewitnesses to the exciting event of seeing a life turned around. So I confess my intent. With God's grace and blessing, more than anything in this world, I want to encourage YOU to have all that God meant for you to have when He placed you on this planet.

— AND WHAT ABOUT YOU? —

Will you join me? If you were arrested for caring and encouraging and brought to court to be tried for Care and Encouragement in the First Degree, would there be enough evidence to convict you?

The following poem, written by the famous author Anonymous, really got my attention. Would you read this carefully and see which group you would choose as your own?

— WHICH AM I? —

I watched them tear a building down, a gang of men in my
hometown;
With a "Heave," and a "Whoa," and a "Yes! Yes!" yell,
they swung a beam and a side wall fell.

And I asked the foreman, "Are these men as skilled,
As the men you'd use if you had to build?"
He gave a laugh and said, "No, indeed!
Just common labor is all I need;
For I can destroy in a day or two
What builders have taken a year to do."

And I thought to myself, as I walked away;
"Which of these role's am I willing to play?
Am I a builder who works with care,
measuring life by the rule and the square?
Am I shaping my deeds to a well made plan
Patiently doing the best I can?
Or am I a wrecker, who walks the town,
content with the labor of tearing down?"

I Can. You Can Too!

Will I be the one tearing down,
As I carelessly make my way around?
Or will I be the one building with care,
So that my community will be a little better,
Just because I was there.

Thank you for staying with me. Thank you, in advance, for using the ideas in this book to better your life. I look forward to seeing you in my travels. If not, then be sure and pick up the 20th Anniversary Special of this book. It will be available in January, 2007, God willing! And please remember: *I CAN*. **And Yes, I Bee**lieve **You Can too!**

— ABOUT THE AUTHOR —

Mamie McCullough is one of the country's most popular motivational speakers and authors. She addresses thousands each year through her seminars and keynote engagements: speaking to churches, schools, and businesses. She has written school programs and authored several books.

Mamie worked with Zig Ziglar for 10 years as his Director of Education. She shares life-changing principles that are instrumental in providing strategies, ideas, suggestions, insights, and facts on how to be the best you can be. She is an encourager, author, speaker, wife, and mother, and feels her greatest achievement in life was receiving her M.A.M.A. degree.

Mamie would like to send you a free copy of her newsletter, "The Encourager." Write for your copy today.

Mamie McCullough & Associates

305 Spring Creek Village

Dallas, TX 75248

For information regarding Mamie speaking
to your organization call:

1-800-255-4226.

Additional copies of this book and other titles by
Mamie McCullough are available
from your local bookstore.

Mama's Rules for Livin' Special Gift Edition

Mama's Rules for Livin'

Rules for Success

Get It Together

I Wish I Had Someone to Take Up For Me

Honor Books
Tulsa, Oklahoma

I Can. You Can Too!